SL04464

CRAFTS

9k

SL04464

CRAFTS

Animals To Appliqué

Charlyne Jaffe Stewart

Sterling Publishing Co., Inc.   New York

ACKNOWLEDGMENTS

○ Thanks to my family members for help with all aspects of assembling this book. Special thanks to my husband, Ralph, for his technical advice, son Gary for his inspiration for *Rhinos on Record*, and my son Mark for his inspiration for *Checkmate*.

○ To Alice Leeds for valuable advice and proofreading.

○ To Harris Publications for allowing me to use *Checkmate*, which appeared in a slightly different form in *Quilt Magazine* in 1982.

○ To PJS Publications for allowing me to use the Rooster Study for a quilt. Article photo reprinted with permission of PJS Publications, Inc., Peoria, Illinois, copyright 1983, *Crafts Magazine*.

○ To Wallace-Homestead Book Company for allowing me to use *Cats at Work*, which appeared in my book *Snowflakes in the Sun* in 1986.

○ To the California Afro-American Museum, the Craft and Folk Art Museum of Los Angeles, the U.C.L.A. Museum of Cultural History, the Shelburne Museum of Shelburne, Vermont, and the Boston Museum of Fine Arts, for assistance in assembling works for the Inspirations Section.

○ To all of the artists who generously contributed their work to the Inspirations Section.

○ To Roland Freeman, who made *Memories of Life on the Farm* available for the Inspirations Section.

○ To Sterling Publishing Company for transforming a manuscript into a book.

Library of Congress Cataloging-in-Publication Data

Stewart, Charlyne Jaffe.
    Animals to appliqué / Charlyne Jaffe Stewart.
      p. cm.
    Includes index.
    ISBN 0-8069-6761-7.—ISBN 0-8069-6760-9 (pbk.)
      1. Appliqué—Patterns. 2. Quilting—Patterns. 3. Decoration and ornament—Animal forms. I. Title.
TT779.S68   1989
746.44′5—dc19

           88-32518
           CIP

Contents

Introduction

Illus. 1. Detail of Snowbunnies *quilt by the author.*

Animals to Appliqué is primarily a book of animal patterns and projects for the quilting enthusiast to appliqué. The patterns are all simple shapes, easy enough for any beginner to attempt with the assurance of satisfying results. They are also basic enough for the more experienced quilter to embellish with additional details or to adapt to individual design plans.

You will find complete projects with the step-by-step directions, diagrams and patterns needed to make many different bed, crib, and wall quilts as well as a set of pillows, a tote bag, a padded box, and a windsock. Ideas for making your own patterns, along with layouts and techniques to consider using, are also given. Many techniques, including some that may be new to you, are demonstrated.

Several sources of inspiration, from other lands and other quilters, are presented to spark your own original designs. Seeing the work of other quilters who use animal imagery in their quilts may well motivate you to try your hand at original work.

Many categories of subject matter, such as fans, stars, baskets, trees, and houses, to name a few, are all popular among quilters. Animals are another, very special category. Animals give us food, clothing, warmth, comfort, and friendship. Appliqué is special, too. It's an easy, forgiving technique. It does a full range of work, from repairing tears to painting fabric pictures. It is so versatile that you can do it by hand, by machine, or in combination; direct or reverse appliqué; flat or padded; alone or accompanied by piecing, painting and embroidery.

I hope *Animals to Appliqué* shows you many ways to place your valued animal friends—whether factual, fictional or fanciful—on a quilt.

Part One: Inspirations

Illus. 2. Mola from the author's collection demonstrates reverse appliqué. Photo by Michael Heilig.

Ideas are everywhere. Even if you don't live on a farm, work at the zoo, or share your space with a pet, there are animals close at hand. Stuffed toys, ceramic, wood, and metal representations, plus those lovable characters in storybooks, can be the starting point for a quilting project.

Begin by looking into your life and interests for clues. Almost every area of life is filled with animals and a subject for a quilt. Many industries use an animal as their salesman—is your company one of them? Are you a sports fan? Many teams, amateur and professional, use an animal to represent them, no doubt hoping to emulate some of the strengths of the mascot. Animals are often used in fashion: owls, pigs, cows, Scottie dogs, or bears are found on everything from dresses to drinking glasses.

Outings to the countryside, county fairs, zoos, marine parks, aviaries, horse, dog, and cat shows, parades, and circuses spawn ideas. While you are enjoying yourself, take a few photos. Make some notes and sketches, too.

In this section, I would like to focus on three areas of special interest to quilters—ethnic textiles from foreign countries; combining traditional pieced block patterns with appliqué; and the work of other quilters.

Textile Arts from Faraway Places

As practitioners of the needle arts, many of us look to other lands with long textile traditions for both information and inspiration. Artful hands produce treasures, each linked to its own culture. Generations of artists have created designs pared down to the essentials, worked out in a complex fashion with astounding skill and ingenuity. Sometimes these treasures have a symbolic meaning to the culture they do not have for us. I feel it is almost impossible to copy these works. We can, however, take one or more elements and simplify the detailing. Then, it becomes possible to transform a foreign idea into a domestic project. If we do our own interpretation and work at our own level of skill, an exciting project with personal meaning can be created.

Every country has its own animal images, design elements, materials, and methods of producing needlework. The country you choose to study might be one that is part of your international heritage, a place you have visited or would like to visit, or simply a country which produces needlework you greatly admire. Here are a few examples of textile work from other countries that have inspired me.

PANAMA

Since we are particularly interested in appliqué, we can learn from the unique folk art of the Kuna (or Cuna) Indians living in the San Blas Islands of Panama. Molas are the cloth panels incorporated into the women's blouses. They are executed in reverse appliqué and direct hand appliqué with touches of embroidery. Many colors are used in these small fabric masterpieces. The tiny stitches have to be seen to be believed. Mola makers work the entire background and foreground with their characteristic tiny slashes of color.

To demonstrate how I would take an element from a mola and simplify it, I selected a bird design that repeats from one of the molas in my collection. The bird has been made into a template, found in the Templates Section on page 74. A quilt could be made by working repeated blocks in contrasting colors. The intricate details which fill the entire mola are thus simplified for the quilt.

Illus. 3. Possible set for a mola-inspired quilt.

Illus. 4. King Tut's Toys, a 54" by 66" quilt by the author. Hand-appliquéd, embroidered, and quilted. Photo by Michael Heilig.

Illus. 5. Japanese carp windsock.

Illus. 6. Fish Flying, a 41" by 68", hand-appliquéd wall hanging by the author. Photo by Michael Heilig.

Illus. 7. Pillow with Colombian appliqué, collection of the author. Photo by Michael Heilig.

Illus. 8. Colombian appliqué detailed with embroidery, collection of the author. Photo by Michael Heilig.

EGYPT

Sometimes we are able to "visit" a faraway place through an exhibit. In the late 1970's, the Egyptian Government allowed a small portion of the fabled treasures of Tutankhamen to be seen at selected museums. The exhibition generated a great deal of excitement, drawing large crowds of people, many of whom had never visited a museum before. It also inspired a large number of needleworks done in the style of ancient Egypt. I was one of the many quiltmakers to mark this very special occasion by making a quilt.

I used the catalogue from the exhibition, which I was able to attend three times, as a reference to plan my design. From the many animal representations I viewed, I chose a falcon, a scarab (beetle) and a leopard head. A lotus flower and two religious symbols, the ankh and the shen, completed the design. I thought that using polished cottons and gold-colored perle cotton to couch the edges of the appliquéd figures would suggest the golden, jewelled nature of the exhibition. The entire background was filled with echo quilting to imitate the sheen given off by the treasures themselves. The exhibition came and went, but my quilt remains as a very personal souvenir.

JAPAN

Having a fondness for things that move, such as kites, windsocks, and mobiles, I have always enjoyed seeing the carp windsocks flying in the wind in front of many of the Japanese stores in the Los Angeles area. In Japan, these flying carp are not only an eye-catching decoration, but symbols of courage and robust health. Families with male offspring mark the celebration of the Festival for Boys by flying these fish on high, one for each son.

Seeing the carp was a springboard for one of my ideas. I began my design for a wall hanging with a simple sketch, changed many times, to give myself an idea of what my project would look like before I began to work in cloth. I teamed the carp with a triangular kite and a box kite made up in strip piecing to look three-dimensional. One extra layer of batting was used under the carp and the other two kites, as well as the circle, to add relief. The kite strings were made with couched yarn strands. As for the quilting design, I drew a series of triangles of various sizes and shapes filled with parallel lines, marking with a ruler and pencil as I went along.

COLOMBIA

Colombia is well known for its charming pictorial appliquéd scenes of pastoral life. Worked entirely by hand, with touches of embroidery, these bits of fabric are filled with animals, people, buildings, trees, flowers and sky scenery. The examples shown here are cheerfully colored and filled with bright fabric and embroidery floss detail.

Illus. 9. A darnia (quilt cover) made in Kutch, India, by a Dhebaria Rabari girl for her dowry. Hand-appliquéd elephants, birds and a single horse are framed with a shisha (mirror) embroidered border. Photo by Antonia Graeber, courtesy U.C.L.A. Museum of Cultural History.

INDIA

Though there is an abundance of outstanding needle-work from India, my favorite pieces contain small bits of glass mirrors incorporated into embroidered appliqué designs (shisha). The combination of two such dissimilar materials—glass and cloth—into luxurious glittering projects that are not only durable but washable is reason enough for me to use mirrors whenever I can. Just as the Japanese carp windsocks were the starting point for my *Fish Flying* quilt, the Indian darnia (quilt cover) shown here is the inspiration for a windsock. As you can imagine, mirror embroidery is especially beautiful when it is moving. (See the Techniques Section for shisha embroidery, and the Projects Section for instructions on how to make the Shisha Embroidered Elephant Windsock.)

Illus. 10. Design for Bear's Paw Quilt *with bear appliqués.*

Traditional Block Patterns

There are thousands of pieced block patterns invented by quiltmakers to add an artistic component to a utilitarian craft. It is the design legacy left to us by the quiltmakers of the past, and constantly revised by contemporary contributors. There are many, many ways we can use this legacy to create quilts with animal motifs.

The names of the block patterns are as intriguing as the patterns themselves. Some reflect everyday domestic experience, historical events, natural phenomena, geographic identification and more. Among the many are patterns with animals in their names, such as Bear's Track, Goose Tracks, and Flying Geese. These recall an earlier time, when many people in the United States were engaged in farming or located in the wilderness. These blocks are often an abstraction of real birds and beasts. How about com-

bining an appliquéd pictorial animal representation with the geometric image of its namesake pieced block? They can be combined in a variety of ways. The appliquéd animals can be used as centerpieces, on borders, alternating with vertical, horizontal, or diagonal block patterns, or in collage settings.

The *Bear's Paw Quilt*, detailed in the Projects Section, is an example of one way to combine appliquéd animals with a block pattern. Taking my clue from the "Bear's Track" pattern, I enlarged the block to make room for the bears. Since it is not necessary to confine oneself to "staying within the lines," I let the large bears extend beyond their background squares. Smaller bears decorate the top and bottom borders. The pattern for the bear can be found in the Templates Section, and instructions for the quilt in the Projects Section.

Illus. 11. Design for Scrappy Monkeys *crazy quilt.*

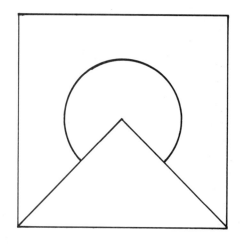

Illus. 12. "Moon Over the Mountain" is a traditional block pattern.

Illus. 13. "Moon Over the Mountain" transformed into sketch for Caravans Quilt.

Illus. 11–14 are sketches for other ideas, showing how you can combine appliqué, pieced work, and a template from the Templates Section.

Another approach to using pieced block patterns is to make a visual connection to an animal. Most quilters have a collection of block patterns that are referred to when ideas for new projects are needed. One of the symptoms of quiltmania is an irresistible urge to spend hour upon hour leafing through this growing collection of block patterns. Each quilter has his or her favorites. The next time you go through your collection, see if you make a connection with an animal.

For example, "Moon Over the Mountain" is a very simple block. It has many possibilities, suggesting different mental images to different people. You might see your vacation home in the mountains, or the moon coming over the top of a skyscraper, or another image altogether. Whenever I look at "Moon Over the Mountain" I see pyramids. The "Caravans" quilt sketched here is one way to develop a design. I have made the pyramids three-dimensional by angling a triangular piece to show two sides. The camels are joined to suggest a caravan travelling through the desert. The pattern for the camel can be found in the Templates Section on page 75.

Illus. 14. Sketch for appliquéd and pieced quilt using cow template.

Illus. 15. An alternate sketch, Dairy Checkers Quilt, *detailed in Projects Section.*

Illus. 16. Carousel Horses Wall Quilt *from Projects Section, showing another combination of animal appliqué and pieced work.*

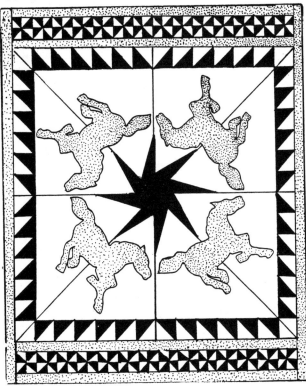

Using block patterns with or without a connection to the appliqué animal may improve your quilt design. First of all, it is fun to combine piecing with appliqué. It gives you an opportunity to do more than one technique. Visually, the combination enhances each component. The geometric straight-line quality of one sets off the curved form of the other and makes exciting contrasts. A few squares, strips, or triangles can do wonders for a simple appliqué. Conversely, the appliqué animals can do the same for a design of single shapes or pieced blocks.

The *Carousel Horses Wall Quilt* in the Projects Section is a good example of this. Four horses are illustrated with four triangle patterns. Each element is easy to do individually. Together, the result is complex and certainly more interesting than if each was used alone. The drawing for a "Scrappy Monkeys" quilt shown here suggests how to combine an appliquéd animal with crazy patchwork.

The Work of Other Quilters

I can't think of anything that gives quilting enthusiasts more inspiration than seeing the work of other quilters, past and present. A visit to a quilt show at a museum or one presented by a local guild must send many a viewer home with an irresistible urge to begin a project of their own. In this section, quilts with animal imagery are presented to demonstrate just a few of the inventive ways that animals can be used in quilts.

Antique quilts from two museum collections provide a glimpse into the past. Four quilts from the Shelburne Museum in Vermont and one from the Boston Museum of Fine Arts show imaginative approaches to using appliquéd animals in quilt designs.

These artists used the familiar animals seen in everyday life as their models, and one of the artists added exotic wild beasts copied from a picture book. The animals are a prominent part of the quilt, or share space with people, plants and flowers, crazy patchwork and pieced work.

Many contemporary quiltmakers contribute their work. Each quilt is a unique expression of something its creator wanted to capture in fabric. A brief history of each quilt provides clues to just what inspired it and the meaning it has to its maker. Some of the artists tell us about the working methods they use to convert ideas into quilts.

Antique Quilts

CAPTAIN MAY—MEXICAN WAR QUILT

This 1850 quilt is thought to have been made by a member of the Noll family of Montgomery County, Maryland. The appliqués in this album-type quilt show designs of floral forms, animals, miscellaneous cutouts, and traditional wreaths. Horses, deer, a cow, chickens, and birds are among the animals displayed. Red, yellow-orange, and green-black calico are used for the appliqués on a white muslin background.

The mounted figure, left of center, represents the charge of Captain May at the battle of Resaca de la Palma during the Mexican War and was adapted from a lithograph by Nathaniel Currier. Captain May had captured the whole of the enemy's cannon and took General La Vega prisoner of war.

LYDIA STAFFORD QUILT

Sometime in the mid-Nineteenth Century Lydia Stafford made this patriotic eagle quilt for her hope chest. She lived in Vermont and later married Warren Barstow, who was a veteran of the War of 1812.

The quilt is worked in both appliqué and patchwork; the eagles are red calico with wings of print and plain calico. The shield/bodies look as though they may have been done as reverse appliqué. They are bordered by strips of triangular patchwork in pale green, red, and yellow. Six-pointed stars of red and yellow calico are placed in each corner of the eagle squares. Each eagle holds three arrows in his left talon and a red ribbon in his beak.

The quilting follows the swag and tassel design held in place by a somewhat more peaceful flock of birds. The repeated eagle blocks are worked in a diamond quilting pattern.

Illus. 19. Haskins Crazy Quilt, *Photo by Einars J. Mengis, staff photographer, courtesy Shelburne Museum, Inc.*

HASKINS CRAZY QUILT

This quilt was made about 1865 by a member of the Haskins family of Granville, Vermont. It is an elaborate crazy quilt composed of 42 blocks. The largest patch in each has an appliquéd animal or human figure. Most of the animals, such as beaver, deer, and farm animals, are those the family saw in everyday life. The exotic beasts, including a camel, elephant, tiger, and giraffe, were copied from an animal picture book similar to one issued by a Brattleboro, Vermont, printer in 1845.

The human figures represent various members of the Haskins family, except the bearded man in the upper right-hand corner block who is thought to represent Abraham Lincoln.

Illus. 20. Quilt by Harriet Powers, 69" by 105". Photo courtesy Museum of Fine Arts, Boston, M. & M. Karolik Collection.

HARRIET POWERS BIBLE QUILT

Harriet Powers (1837–1911) was a former slave from Athens, Georgia. She created appliquéd quilts that reflected her African heritage and Christian experience. She achieved recognition during her lifetime in the following way. Hard times forced the sale of her first quilt. She sold it to a white woman, Jennie Smith, who had long admired it. Mrs. Powers parted with her precious creation, with great reluctance, for $5.00 and Jennie Smith's promise of all future scraps. Mrs. Powers returned several times to visit her quilt.

This first quilt was displayed in Atlanta in 1895 at the Cotton States Exhibition. Due to this exposure, Harriet Powers received a commission for the quilt shown above. This commissioned quilt, made between 1895 and 1898, depicts scenes from the Bible, including the Creation of the Animals, Adam and Eve, the Garden of Eden, and Jonah and the Whale (pictured below). Embroidered details were added in plain and metallic yarns.

Illus. 21–23. Enlarged quilt blocks.

Illus. 24. Pieced and appliquéd quilt made before 1865. Photo courtesy Shelburne Museum, Inc.

PRE-CIVIL WAR QUILT

This quilt, thought to be made in New Jersey, dates from before 1865. It was obviously meant to use up small scraps of fabric (many of which are much older than the Civil War period) in the large area of triangular piecing separating the central appliqué and the appliquéd border. Marching and mounted soldiers are displayed in the inner border. In the center medallion, a mixture of peaceful and militant human figures are accompanied by fat complacent doves. These, plus a few hearts and flowers, temper the military images.

Contemporary Quiltmakers

MICHAEL A. CUMMINGS

Cummings began his artistic career as a painter. A banner-making workshop led by Norman LaLiberté gave him instruction in sewing and increased his interest in working with fabric. His first work was very crude. All attempts to get others to do the sewing were met with either absolute refusals or exorbitant prices. He consulted some books and improved his technique. When the size of his pieces began to grow to 4' × 6', it was time to purchase a sewing machine and learn a new skill.

"My wall hangings are very large. They all tell a story from Afro-American folklore, real events, or personal experience. I think of them as collages of fabrics, buttons, feathers, silver and gold threads, and textile paints. I don't do any sketching, but cut all the shapes directly from the fabric. I use a combination of hand and machine stitching."

The Baby Quilt shown was made for the first child of a couple in New York. The design combines an African animal form, a flower and the sun. The three forms are repeated in the twelve blocks with changes in color and variation of the patterns.

"Springtime in Memphis" is a series of four quilts documenting a trip made to that city in 1979. "Going to that part of the country was an emotional experience, because of all the real and unreal images I carried with me.

"The quilt *At Night* [see Color Section, page A] shows a rural landscape at night. Night birds and spirits (represented by white human forms) and other images fill the sky. According to Haitian mythology the white forms represent invisible spirits. A rocket ship, filled with Egyptians, is speeding across the sky. *The Cross* is part of the Memphis series. In it, I introduce the Holy Cross, which is so much a part of southern experience. The Mississippi River is represented in the blue vertical bands of color. While working on the quilt, I thought about all the black bodies that have been found in this famous river. Consequently, I decided to represent that sad part of black history with human forms. Fish and birds complete the design. The birds in the air symbolize peace and love."

Illus. 25. (Top right) The Cross, *50" by 70", made in 1979 by Michael Cummings.*

Illus. 26. (Bottom right) Baby Quilt, *4' by 7', made in 1977 by Michael Cummings.*

Illus. 27. Fisheating Creek, *48" by 54", made by Jean Eitel in 1987, has crazy quilt piecing and appliquéd cotton calicos and chintz fabrics. Also see Color Section, page A.*

JEAN EITEL

Jean Eitel is a wife and mother who is active in community projects at her home in Florida, and an Episcopalian deacon working primarily with troubled or homeless teenagers. She is well known in the quilting world as the author of *Creative Quiltmaking in the Mandala Tradition* (Chilton, 1985), and the editor of the quilting magazines *Quilt, Country Quilts, Quilt Almanac,* and *Old Fashioned Patchwork.* She travels to quilt guilds throughout the United States to give programs and workshops on quilting and gather material for the magazines, and has taught at the Great American Quilt Festival and the Quilt Festival in Houston.

Fisheating Creek appeared in the 1987 summer edition of *Quilt Magazine.* "In all of creation, the pelican is my favorite bird. There is a whole flock of them living near our home, and I have the pleasure of watching them swoop down for their fish dinner any evening I choose. Also, the pelican is a medieval symbol for piety, and I am constantly working to achieve piety in my life."

Illus. 28. Backyard Bliss, *87¼" by 80", has painted and appliquéd fabric with machine stitching, © by Nancy Erickson in 1984.*

NANCY N. ERICKSON

Nancy Erickson is an artist working in Missoula, Montana, who makes quilts featuring animals, or animals in the company of a female nude. Before teaching herself to quilt, she studied painting, and prior to that, she did undergraduate work in zoology. Though paints or other materials might work as well to make her ideas materialize, fabrics are used for their versatility and adaptability to her large pieces. Her ideas are skilfully sketched, and then transferred into large areas of vividly colored satins, velvets, muslins, etc., which are painted and stitched.

The quilts highlight many animals, including rabbits, wild cats such as leopards and lions, and in two of her series, the capybara. According to one animal handbook, the capybara is the largest of the rodent family, about four feet long, native to South America. This little-known creature has two endearing qualities: It is both gregarious and inoffensive. Nancy Erickson's capybaras comment on her feelings about the precarious state of the environment. (Also see Color Section, page A.)

Illus. 29. Moon Coming Out, *66″ by 49½″, was made by Nancy Erickson (© 1982) of painted satin, cotton, and machine stitching as a commission for Ruth Hoerni. Photo by the artist.*

Illus. 30. Sinking T.V. and Fish, *52½″ × 36″, painted velvet, satin and cotton, machine applique, © 1983 by Nancy Erickson. Photo courtesy the artist.*

Illus. 31. Fish and Chicks, *7' by 7', made by Therese May in 1986 of stitched fabric and acrylic paint.*

THERESE MAY

"I decided to be an artist when I was five. While growing up I did a lot of drawing, painting and sewing. In my undergraduate years at Wisconsin, I pretty much thought of myself as a painter. Then, as a young wife and mother in 1965, I began sewing instead of painting. My quilts were very traditional at first (lots of squares and triangles). Gradually they became more innovative and more painterly. From 1969 to 1977 I made quilts mainly based on photographic images. At that point, I was ready for a change.

"In 1978, my thinking and feelings began to transform and I started to paint again, using fantasy animal and plant imagery. I felt a wonderful freedom, but found that I was divided between the two media, wanting to continue painting, but not wanting to give up quiltmaking. Eventually, in 1983, I began to combine the two by using the fantasy imagery on the quilts and then painting on the finished surface.

"When doing my appliqué process, I like to refrain from clipping the threads so that a very nice network of texture builds and adds interest. Also, I like the idea of making a finished, complete quilt with lots of hours of work in it and then just painting right on that surface. It is a real risk and truly an exciting aspect of quiltmaking for me.

"I like to work in series because I learn so much more in the process with numerous pieces than I do with a single piece."

The examples of May's work that are shown are part of a series of 21 quilts she calls "The Imperfect Quilts" (to combat perfectionism), which are painted with acrylic paints. See Color Section, page D, also.

Illus. 32. (Left) Tropical Fish, 29" by 29", stitched fabric and acrylic paint by Therese May, 1986.

Illus. 33. (Below) Connecting Animals, 41" by 45", stitched fabric and acrylic paint by Therese May, 1986.

Illus. 34. Las Mariposas, *39" by 39", by Charlotte Patera, 1985.*

CHARLOTTE PATERA

Needle artist and designer Charlotte Patera is intrigued by the molas of the Kuna Indians of the San Blas Islands of Panama. Three visits to the islands and a period of time living with a Kuna family have made it possible for her to study the molas thoroughly. To share the variety of mola-making techniques of the Kunas, she has taught many workshops and presented slide programs to a growing number of mola lovers. She has written *Cutwork Appliqué* and *Mola Making* for New Century Publishers, detailing her extensive knowledge of the subject.

The aptly named quilt *Kuna Echos* (see Color Section, page A) complements Charlotte Patera's mola collection, which hangs on the walls of her bedroom. She used some of the animals shown in the molas, using outlines only. "The outlines, or channels, are created by cutting the fabric without removing any of

it and then stitching down both cut edges. Though there are many different mola techniques that then follow, every traditional mola begins with a channel. In this quilt, I used the tandem method for some of them. In other words, I cut two colors at one time (black and coral), then transposed the cut figure and the background piece that surrounded each figure over a foundation of turquoise. After every edge was turned over, the outline, or channel, was formed of the turquoise."

In *Las Mariposas* she wanted to show how one figure could be decorated in nine different Kuna Indian ways. The outlines were created as a channel either with light yellow over dark yellow, or dark yellow over white. She then used the various double appliqué details on each of seven of them, reverse appliqué with inlay triangles on one, and single appliqué "circles" on another.

Illus. 35. Detail of Kuna Echoes, *by Charlotte Patera. See overview of quilt in Color Section, page A.*

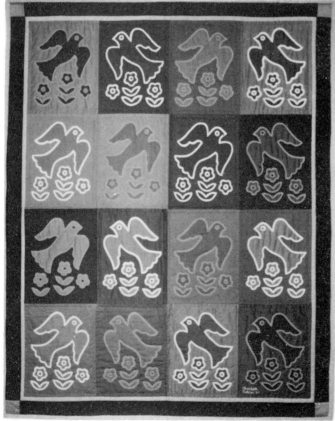

Illus. 36. Skylark, *58″ by 68″, Charlotte Patera, 1983.*

EMMA RUSSELL

Mrs. Russell is a quiltmaker from rural Mississippi. Her 1979 quilt *Memories of Life on the Farm* pictures the animals that were important to her in her early life. Her design expresses the happiness she felt growing up on a farm with the companionship of pets, farm animals, birds and fish. The squirrel, shown at top and left of center, was perched on the tree outside the one-room schoolhouse she attended. Mrs. Russell remembers that this particular squirrel would create quite a commotion if she and the other children neglected to feed it.

Her quilt is part of a collection of Black folk art organized by Roland Freeman. Part of this collection is a travelling quilt exhibition entitled, "Something to Keep You Warm: the Roland Freeman Collection of Quilts Made by African-Americans."

Illus. 37 and 38. Details of Memories of Life on the Farm, *80" by 71", hand-appliquéd, pieced, embroidered and quilted by Emma Russell in 1979. Photos by Roland L. Freeman.*

Illus. 39. Memories of Life on the Farm, *80" by 71", hand-appliquéd, pieced, embroidered and quilted by Emma Russell in 1979. Photo by Roland L. Freeman.*

Illus. 40. Pillow Cat, *14″ by 13″, made of cotton fabrics in 1984 by Laurie Swim. It was designed especially for her book,* The Joy of Quilting, *to inspire beginning quilters to attempt a small, manageable project.*

LAURIE SWIM

Working in Toronto as a designer of fabric murals for corporate and private commercial enterprises, Laurie Swim is also the author of *The Joy of Quilting* (Main Street Press, 1986). She has created movie-set pieces, corporate logos, magazine covers, ads and promotional campaigns. She has shared her skill as a "quiltist"—an artist who makes quilts—in her workshops for adults and children. She uses hand and machine sewing techniques, as well as drawing and painting on a wide range of fabrics. Her work is made up of single and repeated images "to create a mood while remaining close to nature."

Her quilt *The Ugly Duckling* (Color Section, page D) is inspired by the classic Hans Christian Andersen fairy tale. She used many repeats of the same duck traced on white wool with appliquéd silk beaks. The ugly duckling himself is grey velvet, lightly padded and appliquéd. The background is drawn with wax crayons.

The Sheep Look Up was also inspired by a written work, in this case the John Brunner science fiction novel of the same name. It is constructed from cotton and silk. The images of sheep are hand-drawn and quilted with appliquéd heads.

Illus. 41. The Sheep Look Up, *22″ by 33″, 1979, by Laurie Swim.*

Illus. 42. Down the Chulitna, *made by Charlotte Van Zant in 1986. Photo courtesy of the artist.*

CHARLOTTE M. VAN ZANT

Most of Charlotte Van Zant's work is large scale woven tapestry commissions for public buildings, though she is venturing into quilts.

"My husband is a United States Fish and Wildlife biologist here in Alaska, and he has been doing several years of study on trumpeter swans. I am a licensed rehabilitator for injured wild birds, and often have a goose, owl, swallow, or other bird around the place. It's not surprising that birds are often images in my work. I paint them, weave them, quilt them, and watch them on a daily basis."

Although she frequently uses appliqué as a technique, *Down the Chulitna* has a painted central design with a Seminole strip border, and is machine quilted on cotton fabrics. The quilt was shown in *Quilter's Newsletter Magazine* in 1986.

Part Two: Techniques

Illus. 43. Rooster Study, *a hand-quilted project by the author that appeared in* Crafts Magazine © *1983.*

Most of us have a favorite way to work. Do you like to piece, or do you prefer to appliqué? Do you enjoy making the top, but find the quilting tedious? Perhaps you can't wait to get to the quilting process. For some, it is the reward for assembling the top. Do you prefer the leisurely pace of an heirloom project, or do you seek the almost instantly produced "quickie"? Are you on excellent terms with your sewing machine, or do you lean towards handwork? Do you choose the portable project over the stationary? All of these factors influence our choice of technique, but the result produced takes precedence over all of the other qualities inherent in a working method.

In this chapter a variety of techniques is presented to enable you to convert a simple animal shape into an attractive quilt design. Each of the patterns in the Templates Section can be made in any of the techniques you choose. Lists of equipment and materials you will need to make the projects shown in the book follow with instructions for each technique. Select only those materials you need for your favorite working method(s).

TOOLS

Pencils—#2 light and dark leads
Awl—for piercing cardboard and/or plastic
Craft Knife—for cutting interior lines and/or shapes in templates, cutting illustration board
Pins—long and fine
Needles—quilting #7 to #10, sewing, embroidery, tapestry
Scissors—inexpensive pair for cutting paper
Dressmaker's Scissors—8" sharp blades for fabrics
Embroidery Scissors
Seam Ripper
Thimble
Dressmaker's Carbon
Sewing Machine—a zigzag model for machine appliqué
Open-toe foot for machine appliqué
Walking foot for machine quilting
Rotary Cutter and Mat
Ruler
Yardstick
Tape Measure
T-Square
30°–60°–90° Triangle
Flexible Curve—can be bent into any curve and hold its shape, for marking curved lines
Stretcher Bars—notched wooden bars in varying lengths, put together to make frames for mounting wall hangings or small projects
Iron and Ironing Board
Press Cloth

Illus. 44. Cat Quilt by the author, 39" by 45", uses graphic prints for its effects.

MATERIALS

Cardboard—light, file-folder weight to make templates
Plastic Sheets—to make templates
Illustration Board—medium-weight, as a foundation for the "soft boxes"
Fabrics—cottons in percale-type weights in solids or small prints; blends of cotton-rayon, cotton-polyester, or any tightly woven fabric that will keep its edge for hand appliqué. Add novelties, fragile fabrics, metallics for machine appliqué. Use sheer fabrics such as voile, organza, and dotted swiss for shadow quilting. For corded and raised quilting, buy stable knits, velours, and velveteens. Use unbleached muslin (what U.K. citizens know as "calico"—an inexpensive, shrinkproof cotton fabric) for hand, machine, raised, corded quilting and dye painting. All washable fabrics should be prewashed.
Batting—Use a thin bonded batting for hand quilting, thin to thick batting for machine quilting, and thick batting for making the "soft boxes"
Fibrefill—for raised quilting
Tear-away Paper—for machine appliqué
Iron-on Featherweight Interfacing—for machine appliqué and shadow quilting
Thread—quilting thread, sewing thread
Embroidery Floss—perle cotton #3, #5, #8, cotton and rayon floss
Shisha—mirror bits to attach to embroidered appliqué. Heavy-duty, doubled aluminum pan foil can be substituted.
Yarn—thick and washable for corded quilting

Design

The first step in planning your project is to decide which animal(s) you wish to feature in your design. The next is to find a picture or drawing of that animal in a pose you like. There are many animals from which to choose in the Templates Section. For other choices, look to your home library or to your neighborhood library. If you are fortunate enough to have an encyclopedia, you will find a wide variety of both photographs and outline drawings. Your local library may have several sets of encyclopedias, as well as many volumes on science and natural history. The children's section of the library will have a wide selection of fictional and factual materials on animals. Check out the magazine section. Also ask the reference librarian, if there is one on duty, to point out any special materials that might be of use.

When you have made your selection, trace or photocopy. If the drawing is too small or too large, or not in the exact pose you want, it can be altered, as I will demonstrate.

Before you begin to make any changes, decide on an overall plan. Are you going to use a repeat design, medallion, circular plan, or other type of design? You don't have to have your plan completely worked out, but you must know what kind of background shape and size the animal pattern will have to fill. Many plans will involve a pattern no larger than a sheet of 8½″ × 11″ paper. These are the ones you can adapt with the help of pencil, paper, scissors, and the photocopier at the local printer's or copy shop.

Planning on paper can save you hours of time and money, and make it possible to see your project before you make it. A nice bonus is that your skills as a designer grow with each attempt.

SKETCHING WITH PHOTOCOPIER AND SCISSORS

The photocopier does many things in addition to making copies. Some models enlarge, reduce, or reverse an image. Prior to altering the animal drawing or photograph, the image must be enlarged, reduced or turned in the desired direction. If you are working with a tracing, place it on an opaque sheet of paper and outline it with a soft-tip pen. Look in the Yellow Pages for listings of copy shops or printers that have a photocopier that performs the service you desire. Ask if the machine is working and about the charges involved.

Oftentimes the size you want will take more than one increase or decrease. Each is expressed as a percentage. The shop will charge for each change in size. I've found the price range to be minimal, though increases are slightly more expensive than reductions.

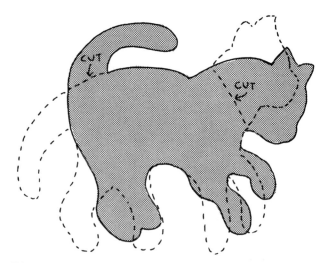

Illus. 45. Cut and glue to make new shapes.

"Reverses" are necessary when you want to change the direction the animal will be facing, or if you want repeats to face each other. Once it is the proper size, the machine will copy the image onto clear plastic. The plastic sheet can be flipped over to the other side to copy the reverse image. I found the charge for this service to be under a dollar.

Spending a small amount of money can save you hours of sketching, trying to enlarge, reduce, or duplicate your animal shape in reverse.

Some shapes are so simple they are easy to draw freehand. For example, fish, bird or cat shapes are not too difficult. All you are after is an outline shape that suggests the chosen animal. Drawing a camel or horse might involve more skill, or more attempts. It never hurts to try. You might surprise yourself. Use a scissors, as well as a pencil, to make changes. If you are starting with a shape that more or less is what you are after, only minor adjustments are necessary. If parts need trimming, follow the contours and cut away. Start by cutting the shape out and placing it on a sheet of paper. If you like one part and not another, cut away what you don't like. Using the good portion as a guide, move it around and trace the outline. Glue the pieces and cut out again. Keep drawing and cutting until the pose is exactly what you want.

COMPOSING REPEATS

The most popular method of designing projects is to make a plan which repeats a single image. There are many variations. Repeats can be identical, with or without frames. Each animal can be cut from the same or different fabric. Animals can face the same direction or face each other, creating a relationship between them. Rows of repeats can be horizontal, vertical, or diagonal. They can also be scattered in a

Illus. 46. Cats at Work, *by the author. The center design was created by folding and cutting in the* snowflake *method. (From* Snowflakes in the Sun, *copyright 1986 by Wallace-Homestead Book Co., Lombard, IL)*

random pattern. The animals combine nicely with pieced blocks, rows, or borders.

When you made your pattern(s), you had a general idea about layout. This is the time to finalize your plan.

MAKING A PAPER PLAN

1. Reduce the size of your animal's pattern. It should be small enough to arrange on a sheet of 8½″ × 11″ paper. As you might have enlarged a small drawing or photo to make your pattern(s), the original, smaller size may be in your possession. Make copies.
2. Cut them out. If the animal is too small or too complicated, and therefore too difficult to cut out, cut a small square or free-form shape to represent it.
3. Arrange these on the graph paper. Move them around, trying several groupings. When you get an arrangement you like, glue it in place.

4. Divide the space. Draw in pieced sections or add lines to denote frames, borders, or other divisions.
5. Color areas with a black or grey pencil, making dots, lines, and free-form squiggles to indicate how different fabrics might be used.
6. Use correcting fluid to make changes and corrections, or to clean up lines.
7. Put the design away for a day and look at it again with a fresh eye.
8. Retain the parts that are pleasing and cut away those that are not.
9. Draw, cut, rearrange, and reglue.
10. If you arrive at more than one design you would like to translate into a quilt, use the best one. Save the other(s) for another time.

The Projects Section has many sample arrangements that were arrived at by using the method described.

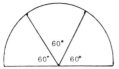

FOLD IN HALF   FOLD TO THE RIGHT   FOLD TO THE LEFT

Illus. 47. Arranging repeats in a circle. Above: folding into 60° sections. Right: one design repeated. Far right: two designs alternated.

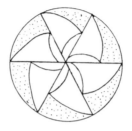
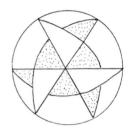

ARRANGING REPEATS IN A CIRCLE

A circular space is created when the animal repeats are arranged in a ring. There are several ways to divide the space to enhance the animal shapes.

Dividing by Folding a Circle into Equal Wedges and Subdividing by Drawing Curved Lines.
1. Cut a paper circle.
2. Fold it into six equal sections; use a protractor to divide the space into six 60° sections and follow the folding procedure in Illus. 47.
3. Open. Use curved lines drawn freehand, or with a flexible curve, to divide each wedge. Arrange the elements in a repeated or alternating sequence around the circle.
4. After arriving at a central design you like, enlarge it to scale.
5. For piecing, make templates by tracing each wedge design onto see-through plastic. Number each section. Cut apart.

Dividing By "Snowflake" Method: Folding a Circle into Wedges and Cutting. This procedure is similar to the previous one except that the design is cut instead of drawn. A circle is cut out and then folded into sixths. Parts are cut out to make a central design, which can be appliquéd by hand or machine. The design can be cut freely, or you may prefer to draw some lines to serve as a guide for the cutting.

Dividing a Circle into Strips. Another approach to filling a central circle is to make a strip-pieced composition, as is shown in Illus. 76 on page 48. (See the section on cutting and sewing freely in the Techniques Section.)
1. Cut and stitch together a series of fabric strips.
2. Recut and insert contrasting colored strips.
3. Cut into a circle.
4. Appliqué to background and add other appliquéd parts, if desired.

FOLD IN HALF

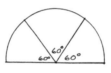

FOLD TO THE RIGHT

TO THE LEFT

DRAW A DESIGN AND CUT OUT

Illus. 48. The snowflake method.

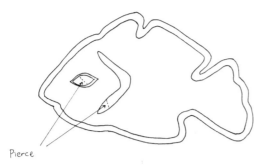

Illus. 49. Pierce interior shapes with awl to start the cut.

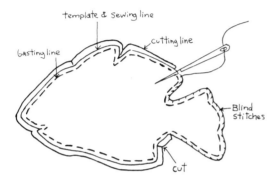

Illus. 50. The Hawaiian method of hand appliqué.

Illus. 51. Shapes can be cut apart and divided into smaller shapes.

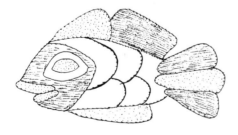

Illus. 52. Other fabrics can be appliquéd on top, layer over layer.

Making Templates

Start with a simple animal shape. Trace it from this book, other sources, or draw your own onto light-weight cardboard. File-folder cardboard is the perfect weight. It cuts easily and holds its edge for several uses. For a permanent template, use see-through plastic. If interior lines and/or shapes need to be cut out, pierce the plastic with a thick needle or awl to start the cut. Insert a craft knife or scissors to finish. Make all templates actual size. For some techniques such as machine appliqué, no seam allowance is added: The edge of the template is the cutting line. In other techniques such as hand appliqué the cutting line is ¼″ out from the template.

Hand Appliqué

Place the template on the wrong side of the fabric. Mark the template outline with a #2 pencil. This is the sewing line. Mark as many animal shapes as required and remember to cut ⅛″ to ¼″ outside the drawn line to allow the turn-under allowance. I like to use the Hawaiian method to turn under the edge on cotton fabrics or blends that are closely woven and keep their edge.

1. Baste approximately ¼″ inside the sewing line to anchor the appliqué pieces to the ground fabric.

2. Make a tiny starting cut ⅛″ inch long from the outside perpendicular to the sewing line. Make extra-small cuts into the sewing lines where the design calls for a sharp inward turn (as in the top of Illus. 50 at the fins) to make it easier to turn the edge under. Use your needle to help push the fabric edge under as you go; the basting line will act as a stop. Make a small, almost invisible series of blind stitches along the edge, matching the thread color to the appliqué piece.

3. Remove the basting stitches. Press.

Other methods can be used. Pressing the seam allowance with an iron over a template to turn the edge is one way. The shape can also be finger-pressed as you go and basted to the ground. Experienced needleworkers can simply pin the shape to the ground and turn the edge under as they sew a small section at a time, without doing any basting at all. It is a matter of preference, size, and complexity of the design.

The shape can be cut apart. Cutting the template apart, instead of the fabric, will improve accuracy and the cut-apart shapes can be repeated—exactly.

Other fabrics can be appliquéd to the shape. Pin and baste all the layers together, as if they were one. At spots where they intersect, release a few of the basting stitches. Stitch the bottom layer first, then the ones covering in order from bottom to top. Be sure all raw edges are covered by the top layers.

Machine Appliqué

This method can be used for work that is to be done quickly. It will stand up to heavy use and washing, and lends a bold satin-stitched outline to the animal shapes and interior details.

1. Iron fusible featherweight interfacing to the wrong side of the fabric area to be used, in order to stabilize the fabric and keep it flat while you are stitching on the machine.

2. On the wrong side of the fabric, mark and cut one or more animal shapes. No seam allowance is added for machine appliqué—cut the shapes out right along the line.

3. Pin and/or glue the shape(s) to the ground fabric.

4. Place the tear-away paper under the ground fabric at the area to be appliquéd. This paper will keep the satin stitch flat.

5. Set your sewing machine for a medium-width, open zigzag stitch. Thread color can either be matching or contrasting. Any color thread can be used in the bobbin. Use an open-toe foot to improve visibility.

6. Use the zigzag stitch on the edges to anchor the piece. This firmly bastes the appliqué pieces to the ground.

7. Mark any interior lines desired using a #2 pencil.

8. Re-set your machine for a closed satin stitch that is wider than the preparatory zigzag. Cover the edges and all of the interior lines marked.

9. Tear away the paper inside and outside the shapes. Cut away all loose thread ends. Press.

10. When using designs with multiple fabrics, pin and/or glue smaller sections to the main appliqué. Follow the same procedure.

11. On large projects, I baste all the edges and pieces superimposed. This prevents shifting, despite all the movement involved in this technique.

CRAZY PATCHWORK DONE WITH MACHINE APPLIQUÉ

1. Trace animal shape on the wrong side of lightweight fusible interfacing.

2. Using a #2 pencil, draw lines to break up the space.

3. Number each section. Make a photocopy to act as a placement guide.

4. Cut sections apart and iron each section to the wrong side of its assigned coordinating fabric.

5. Assemble cut fabric pieces on the ground fabric, referring to the photocopy for placement. All the pieces should touch. Pin and/or glue them in place. Baste if desired.

6. Follow the instructions for machine appliqué. Stitch on the line formed by each side of the pieces, catching both sides on all the interior lines. Use the widest setting.

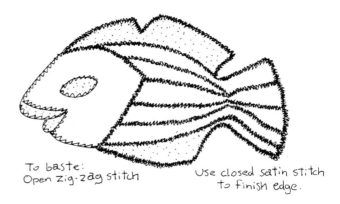

To baste: Open zig-zag stitch

Use closed satin stitch to finish edge.

Illus. 53. Machine appliqué.

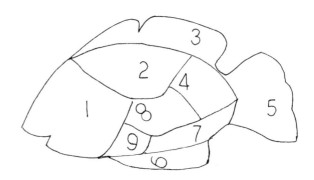

Illus. 54. Draw lines to break up spaces into smaller spaces to make crazy patchwork by machine.

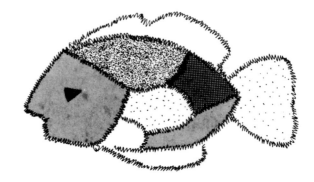

Illus. 55. Machine appliqué crazy patchwork: final result.

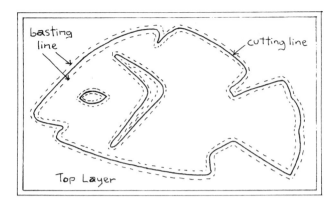

Illus. 56. Reverse appliqué: baste on both sides of cut line to make lines of color.

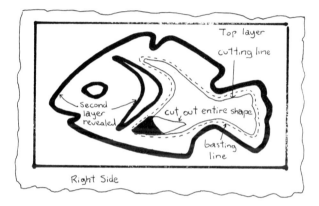

Illus. 57. Several layers can be used. At right: how to cut out a large area.

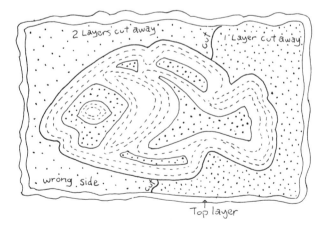

Illus. 58. View of wrong side, showing how fabric is removed from the back to improve ease of quilting.

Reverse Appliqué

This technique is similar to direct hand appliqué. It is used for two or more varicolored layers stacked one on top of the other and reveals areas of the "hidden" layers by cutting and sewing. The photographs of molas or mola-inspired projects in this book, such as those by Charlotte Patera, are all examples of this technique.

1. Prepare a template of the animal shape.

2. Stack the layers of fabric in the order desired. Pin together. This takes some forethought and planning. Do some preliminary experimentation, particularly to see what the order should be and how the colors work together.

3. Trace the outline of the animal shape and any interior lines desired onto the right side of the top fabric layer, using a light or dark #2 pencil—whichever contrasts with the fabric.

4. Make a starting cut on the cutting line; use a straight pin to lift the top layer up from the lower layers. Insert scissors into the starting cut and cut along the line, cutting the top fabric only. *Baste on one side only* to remove a shape and create a large area of the lower fabric's color (Illus. 57, right-hand side). Illus. 57, left-hand side, shows the basting procedure for revealing thick lines of the color of the fabric underneath the top layer; baste ⅛" on *both* sides of the cutting line, cut between the basting lines, and turn fabric under. Take care not to cut into the lower layers.

5. The sewing procedure is the same as for direct hand appliqué. A starting cut up to the sewing line is made. Small, almost invisible, stitches of thread matching the top layer are worked along the sewing line with the blind stitch. Additional cuts in to the sewing line are made as needed, mostly on curves that turn inward. On sharp curves that turn outward, take a few extra stitches to allow for little or no turn-under allowance.

6. Draw outlines of areas to be removed from the next layer. Repeat cutting and stitching procedures. Usually each fabric area exposed is smaller than the previous one. Thick lines are approximately ¼" wide or as determined by the placement of the basting lines.

Several layers can be used in a single design. How many depends on the thickness and softness of the fabric, size of the project, and complexity.

If no quilting will be done, removing excess fabric layers is optional. For quilted work the excess must be cut away, because it is difficult to quilt through several layers at once and make small stitches. Turn the piece to the wrong side. Using a pin, lift one layer at a time and cut away the excess fabric. Leave at least ¼" beyond each stitching line. It might be helpful to mark a cutting line first.

Strip Piecing

There are many ways strip piecing can be utilized to enhance animal shapes. Pieced strips can be inserted within the animal shape or between sections of the background to emphasize the appliquéd areas. A variety of very small, intricate bands of pieced work can be easily and accurately pieced on the sewing machine.

There are two basic methods or approaches to strip piecing. One, the Seminole method, follows formal rules of construction. Strips are cut in designated widths, machine-stitched, recut and restitched one or more times. All seams are carefully matched. This technique, invented by the Seminole Indians of Oklahoma and Florida, has revolutionized quiltmaking. Hours of time are saved without sacrificing the fine results produced by traditional methods. Some quilters who find traditional piecing difficult are able to make all sorts of complicated-looking bands of pieced work with ease.

SEMINOLE STRIP PIECING

Making the strip pattern shown in Illus. 60 is a good demonstration of the technique.
1. Cut three strips of fabric. Use one dark- and two light-colored fabric strips. They must be the same width. Machine-stitch together, allowing a ¼″ seam allowance. Press seams.
2. Cut into strips the same width as the finished width of the central (dark) strip plus ½″ for a seam allowance (¼″ each side).
3. Offset strips by moving one square down for each section. Use a pin through the seam lines to match seams exactly. Stitch. Press seams.
4. Stitch another long strip to each side along the dotted line indicated in Illus. 60, 4A. Press seams and trim excess fabric.

FREE-STYLE METHOD

This method is similar to the previous one. However, these strips can be cut in varying widths. They can be cut in any direction. The seams can match or not match. The approach is very informal.
1. Sew several strips together, of the same or different widths. Use a ¼″ seam allowance. Press seams.
2. Cut in any direction, either perpendicular or on any angle to the seam line. Take special care in handling bias edges. If the edge is long, stay-stitch it with a large machine stitch.
3. Cut additional strips and sew to cut edges.
4. Cut and resew. Repeat as desired to create your design.

The final design shows the dark strip stitched parallel, perpendicular, and at an angle (on the bias) to the pieced strips.

Illus. 59. A Seminole strip inserted into an animal shape.

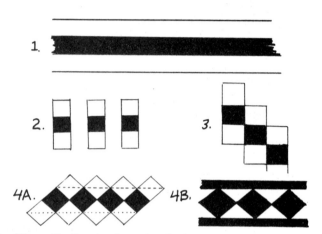

Illus. 60. Seminole strip piecing.

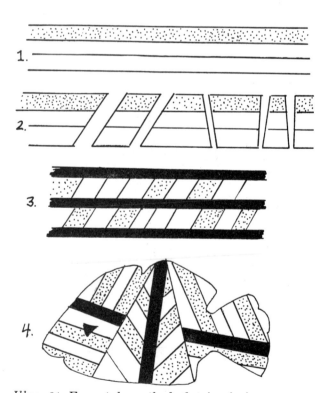

Illus. 61. Free-style method of strip piecing.

Illus. 62. Seminole sampler by the author, machine-pieced with hand-appliquéd animals, machine-quilted.

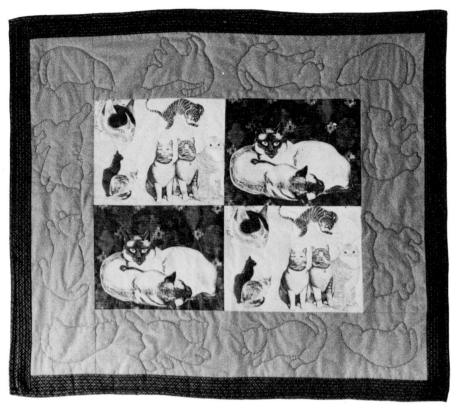

Illus. 63. Copy Cats, *31″ by 36″, by the author.*

Making a Heat Transfer on a Color Copier

An almost instant quilt block can be made by the color copier at your local printer's or copy shop. You can use photographs, drawings, and even found objects (those that are flat). The possibilities are exciting. Here is a method to produce a one-of-a-kind block that is quick and easy. Prior to making any preparations, check on the availability of color copiers. Look in the phone book for listings. Find out the following:

1. Do they have a machine that makes heat transfers for T-shirts? This is the process that will be used, with *your* fabric instead of a T-shirt. If they have a color copier that does heat transfers, continue asking:

2. Is the machine working?

3. Do they have transfer paper in stock for the machine?

4. What is the charge for making each transfer?

5. Is there a quantity discount?

6. What is the charge for applying (ironing on) the transfer to the cloth which you will supply?

7. What type of cloth do they recommend?

8. What are the color choices? (The color settings for the machine are the limiting factor.)

To make the *Copy Cats Quilt* pictured in Illus. 63, I began by arranging some cutouts I had saved from calendars, art posters and greeting cards, onto two 8½″ × 11″ pieces of cardboard covered with fabric. When I arrived at arrangements I liked, I glued the cutouts to the background. When several small images are used to make up the 8½″ × 11″ space, you have the option of cutting them apart and applying them to a background, or keeping them intact. At the copy shop, I requested a full color setting. Other choices were red, blue, or yellow. Though some of the brightness of the original was lost, as well as the sharpness of line, the duplication of the image was good.

Before the heat transfers were made, I requested a plain-paper color copy of each arrangement. This gave me a good idea of what my cloth copies would look like. Then I gave the operator four pieces of white cloth cut 12½″ × 15″, four inches larger than the original blocks. I decided on 100% cotton percale although cotton-polyester mixtures are also suitable. I prewashed and ironed the cloth. The charge was only a few dollars for making and transferring each block. You might choose to pay even less should you decide to have the shop prepare the transfers and iron them on yourself.

Despite a coated surface on the cloth, I found it easy to do the quilting. When you are ready to clean a finished project, remember to use cool water to hand-wash and line-dry. Use a protective cloth when ironing.

Dye Painting on Fabric

This is another way to add details too small to appliqué. The entire shape can be painted and embroidery added, as well as quilted touches. Because there are many products on the market, it is best to follow the label directions and prepare a sample before starting your project. You want to make sure the color is permanent and washable.

1. Transfer the animal shape to fabric that has been washed and ironed. Use dressmaker's carbon, or make a template.
2. Outline with a fine-line permanent marker.
3. Place the fabric in a hoop.
4. Color each area with dye paint, using a brush or applicator. Apply one color at a time. For example, paint all the areas that are purple. Allow them to dry completely. Repeat with the next color, and so on. If two colors do not touch each other, it is all right to paint them without waiting for them to dry.
5. Heat-set with iron or clothes dryer, depending on the product instructions.
6. Wash, if required.

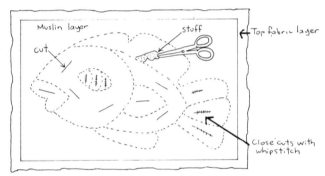

Illus. 64. View of wrong side, demonstrating raised quilting method.

Raised Quilting

Raised quilting is another way to create a raised design, which is especially effective on smaller-shaped projects such as pillows and boxes. However, it may add weight and distort the shape of the fabric.

1. Mark the design on a piece of muslin. Baste to the wrong side of the fabric top.
2. Hand- or machine-stitch on the lines indicated.
3. Using a straight pin to separate the two layers, make a tiny cut in the bottom muslin layer only. Take care not to cut the top layer. Large sections may need more than one cut, depending on the size and shape of the area.
4. Using a small embroidery scissors, stuff a small amount of fibrefill into each compartment formed by the stitching.
5. Stuff lightly or firmly as desired.
6. Close each compartment with a whipstitch.

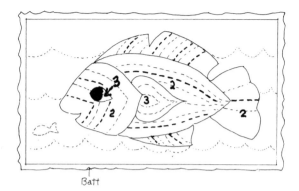

Illus. 65. Padded appliqué.

Padded Appliqué

On designs requiring the illusion of depth, relief levels can be varied by adding additional layers of batting under designated areas to create a raised surface. Begin with the smallest pieces. In Illus. 65, they are the pieces labelled with the number 3, meaning 3 layers of batting. The numbers indicate the layers of batting under those areas. Light lines show sewing that penetrates appliqué only. Heavy lines show quilting that penetrates all layers. They anchor the appliqué figure.

1. For each appliqué shape you wish to pad, cut one layer of thin batting of the same size. In Illus. 65, one layer of batting is cut for the body of the fish, as well as one for the eye and the pectoral fin. Batting and fabric can be cut together. Trim away the seam allowance of ¼″ on the batting layer. Mark the fabric layers for quilting and place on top of the correspondingly shaped batting piece.
2. Following the directions for hand appliqué, attach the smaller pieces to the larger piece. For example, place the small-shaped eye and fin, with batting, on the fish body. Then, quilt on marked quilting lines.
3. Place the larger shape on corresponding layer of batting and cut; then pin and appliqué to the next-larger fabric shape, and so on. For example, place the larger-shaped fish body on the corresponding layer of batting. Appliqué to the background. Quilt on marked lines. As the layers are added to the appliqué design, additional quilting stitches may be added to anchor the piece. (These are indicated on the drawing as heavy lines on the fish body.) These stitches may have to be done one at a time because it may be difficult to penetrate multiple layers.
4. Prepare for quilting: Place a layer of batting on a backing fabric which has been placed right side down. Place the quilt top, right side up, on the batting. Center. Pin and/or baste in place following the general directions for quilting, page 46. Quilt.

Corded Quilting (Trapunto)

This technique is sometimes used in conjunction with raised quilting, or alone to form thick raised lines. The preparation is similar to raised quilting. The design is marked on a piece of muslin and basted to the wrong side of the fabric top. It is important to mark a double line, as evenly spaced as possible. There is an inexpensive and helpful product on the market that is just perfect for marking corded quilting. The Dream Seamer® is available at fabric and quilting shops. It is a tiny metal disc with a hole in the middle. When slipped over a pencil, it makes a parallel line ¼″ away from the line it is following. You can draw your lines freehand, of course, but it makes the work easier to use this device.

1. After making your design on the muslin layer and basting it to the wrong side of the fabric top, hand- or machine-stitch on the lines marked.

2. Thread a large-eyed blunt tapestry needle with a thick yarn. If your project is to be washable, use a yarn that can be washed. Thread the needle with yarn through the channel formed by the two lines. Do not penetrate the top fabric layer.

3. At the turns, bring the needle out from the muslin backing on the wrong side in order to change direction with the needle and to allow a bit of slack to keep the yarn relaxed. This is shown in Illus. 66 as dark loops.

4. Since all work is done on the wrong side and will be hidden when the project is completed, it is not mandatory to be overly neat in cutting thread ends. Knots are acceptable, too.

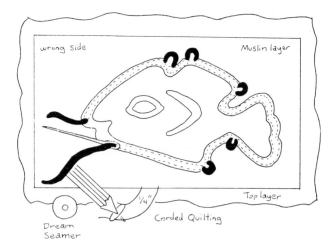

Illus. 66. View of wrong side, demonstrating corded quilting method.

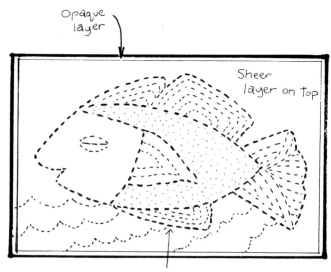

Appliqué between the top and bottom layers.

Illus. 67. Shadow quilting.

Shadow Quilting

In this technique the appliqué is held between two layers of fabric, an opaque layer below and a sheer layer above. Because there is no need to turn under any edges on the appliqué shapes, shadow appliqué projects are quickly completed. The sheer layer which is placed on top of the appliqué not only softens bright colors, but can add a beautiful texture to the surface. All sorts of wonderful sheer fabrics can be used—dotted swiss, lace, and voile, to name just a few.

1. Prepare the template for the appliqué shape. Mark on wrong side of opaque fabric that has been backed with fusible featherweight interfacing. The interfacing helps to seal the edges of the appliqué fabric and stabilize it. The line marked is the cutting line.

2. Cut two pieces of fabric, one opaque, for the background, and one sheer, one inch larger than the designated size and shape of the background area.

3. Place appliqué on opaque background fabric. Pin and/or glue in place. Cover with the sheer layer. Remove pins and repin on top of the sheer layer. Mark all quilting lines on both the appliqué shape and background fabric. Baste. Remove pins.

4. Prepare for quilting and follow the general directions for Hand or Machine Quilting. All appliqué shapes must be quilted on the edges to hold the appliqué in place.

5. Remove basting.

Adding Embroidery

Details too small to appliqué, such as eyes, ears, fins, markings, interior lines, or outlines, can be applied with a needle and thread. Edges can be reinforced as well as decorated. The entire shape can be filled with one or more stitches, or designated areas can be accentuated with a color or texture contrast. Little mirror pieces (shisha) can be attached for a touch of the exotic.

Couching—A thick embroidery thread or several strands are placed along the outside edge of the appliqué. The ends are brought to the wrong side with the help of a large-eyed needle and knotted off. A series of parallel stitches spaced at close intervals over the thick thread holds it in place. This makes a nice decorative edge, reinforces it, and covers up less-than-perfect hand stitching.

Satin Stitch—The area to be covered is outlined with a #2 pencil. Stitches are placed side by side, touching, until the area is filled.

Chain Stitch—Looped stitches are used for outlining or interior lines, and can be used to cover an area when rows are placed side by side.

Blanket (Buttonhole) Stitch—Another looped stitch that will make a decorative and strong edging for appliquéd shapes. For shisha it can also be used to cover the attaching mirror work, when it is closely worked.

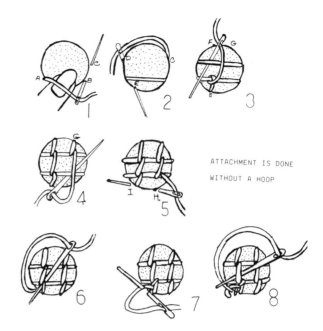

Illus. 69. Shisha embroidery.

Shisha Mirror Embroidery

Work without a hoop. Hold the mirror in place on top of the fabric with your thumb and forefinger. If this is your initial effort, use a bit of thickened white glue under each mirror bit. After a little practice, you will find them easy to attach without glue.

1. Come up at A, down at B, and up at C.
2. Come down at D and up at E.
3. At the intersection, go over, around, and up, making a catching loop. Repeat at the next intersection.
4. Come up at G. Repeat the procedure at the next two intersections.
5. Come down at H and up at I, ready to begin covering the network. You have completed the attaching network.
6. The network may be covered with a closely worked blanket stitch, also known as a buttonhole stitch, or by a variation of the Cretan stitch, more loosely worked, which is illustrated above. One part of the stitch will be worked over the network just completed and the other will go through the background fabric. The tiny stitches on the fabric will be turned so that they are parallel with the edge of the mirror piece. Go over and under the intersection according to Illus. 69.
7. Make a tiny stitch, catching the thread under the needle.
8. Repeat the steps 6 and 7, until the entire network is covered. Bring the thread to the back and knot off.

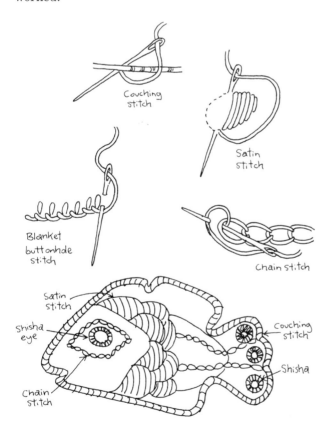

Illus. 68. Embroidery stitches.

Preparing To Quilt

As every quilter knows, quilting is the stitching process that holds the quilt layers—the backing, batting, and top—together. The simple running stitch enhances whatever technique is used to make the top. With an attractive quilting pattern, the quilting can stand all by itself as a method to decorate an entire quilt top or parts of it.

1. If you want to make quilting designs to echo your appliquéd animals, place the template on the quilt top and outline lightly with a #2 pencil. Remove the template and mark any interior lines to be quilted.
2. Prepare for quilting: Cut backing and batting layers 1″ larger than the top. Place the backing fabric right side down, put the batting on the backing and the quilt top on the batting. Center. Pin and/or baste at 4″ to 6″ intervals horizontally and vertically. Baste on the outside edges.

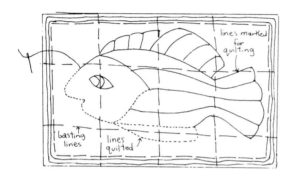

Illus. 70. Quilting by hand.

Hand Quilting

1. Place in quilting frame or hoop. (If the piece is too small for the hoop, machine-baste strips of muslin to make it big enough to fit.)
2. Quilt with either contrasting or matching thread. Use small even running stitches, starting and ending with a back stitch. Clip ends.
3. To make your design outline even more prominent, use embroidery thread and large even stitches with small spaces between them.

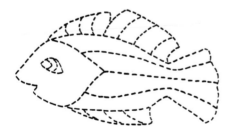

Illus. 71. Finished quilting design.

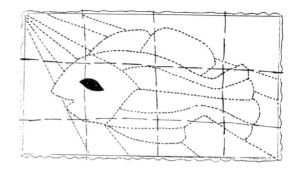

Illus. 72. Machine quilting.

Machine Quilting

Quilting by machine saves time, improves the strength of the project, and is especially easy to do on small projects. The preparation of the three layers for quilting is similar for both hand and machine quilting, but make your basting lines at closer intervals (4″ or closer). This will keep the work flat while you are making all the twists and turns machine-quilted designs may require.

1. Follow the general directions in Preparing To Quilt.
2. Set your sewing machine for a large stitch. Use a walking-foot attachment to make the work easier. Instead of pushing the fabric through the machine as the regular foot does, it "walks on" the fabric. This makes it easy to stitch through the multiple layers, avoiding any bunching or pleating of the backing fabric. (NOTE: You can quilt on your machine without this attachment. Just be sure to loosen your tension.)

Binding-off Projects

1. Cut four binding strips to measure ½″ longer than the two widths and lengths. Piece to make long strips.
2. Bind the long sides first and then the short edges, following Illus. 73; stitch the binding to the right side, ¼″ from edge. Then fold binding into thirds. Stitch ends. Turn to the wrong side.
3. Hand-stitch on the seam line.

Making Hanging Straps

1. Cut five strips 2″ × 5″ from the binding fabric. Fold in half, then each half into quarters. Stitch close to both edges.
2. Fold in half across the length and place at regular intervals, one in the middle and two placed one inch before the outside edge of the hanging. Pin and stitch in place.
3. Bind the top edge, covering the raw edges of the hanging straps. Pull up and tack the straps at the top edge.
4. Insert a dowel rod. Hang.

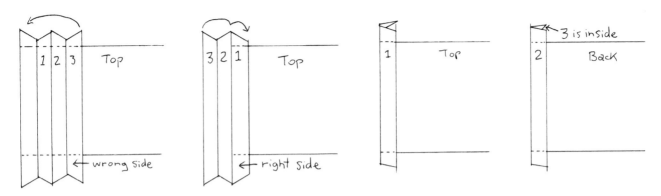

Illus. 73. Binding the sides.

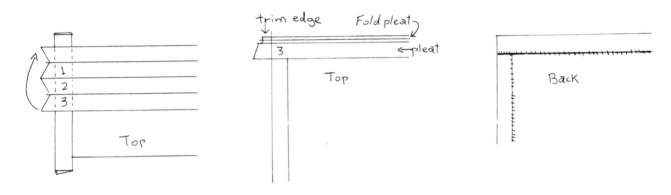

Illus. 74. Finishing corners.

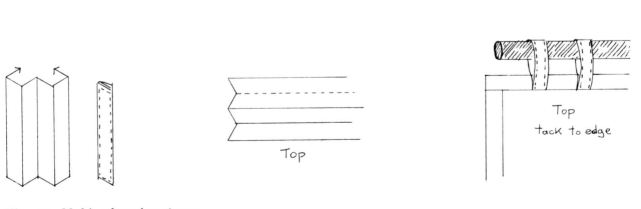

Illus. 75. Making hanging straps.

Part Three: Projects

Illus. 76. Armadillos Aligning, *42" by 42", by the author. It is machine strip-pieced, hand-appliquéd and quilted, and mounted on a larger fabric-covered board.*

A variety of domesticated and wild animals is featured in this section. Several of the techniques explained in the Techniques Section are utilized to make the bed quilts, wall quilts, pillows, bag and box shown. Each animal pattern is suitable for a quilt block. Projects can be used as is or modified to suit your design, or favorite animals can be substituted for those shown.

Throughout the ages people in civilizations as different as the Egyptian and Aztec have kept wild animals in captivity. The London Zoo, which opened its gates in 1829, was the first collection to take a scientific approach. The major part of the collection consisted of dead specimens for scientific study. The staff wore top hats and white trousers. Public interest began to grow after a decision was made to relegate the dead specimens to another institution and to acquire live animals to fill the void. Visitors had to be trained in proper behavior. Keepers were constantly restraining visitors from teasing the animals and playing pranks. Pouring gin into the water troughs was a favorite prank of the Nineteenth Century cut-up. Today millions of people continue to visit zoos, aquariums, and marine parks. Many of them are regular visitors returning time after time to see the monkeys, elephants, lions, tigers, and bears.

Surprising as it may seem, the main purpose of a zoo (short for zoological garden) is not to display animals at all, but to provide an opportunity to study them. When animals are for display only, the presentation is called a menagerie. Combining this with the word *mélange*—"mixture"—the "Melangerie" Wall Hanging is a collection of nine wild animals captured in cloth and thread for display in any of your rooms. The selection is arbitrary, since there are so many choices to be made from an extremely large animal kingdom. For me, making selections for the top and bottom sections was easy. Birds for the top, fish and lizards for the bottom seemed a natural selection. The remaining spaces were filled with a loris, possum, pangolin (spiny anteater), reindeer, elephant, and panda.

Pat's Pet Shop is another layout idea for displaying your or a friend's favorite animals, which can be made up as a gift and customized with the recipient's name.

The *Arabian Horse Quilt* is a combination of a traditionally pieced center surrounded by a border of galloping horses. Arabic Lattice is reputed to be a difficult pattern. Though it is not an easy pattern, it is not all that difficult, either. The majority of the pieces in the block is joined in straight lines. The final piece is fitted to adjacent corners. By joining to one side and then to the other, and by *going up to* and *not into* the seam allowance, any problem can be avoided. A tessellated design, which began as one to be used in a tile or mosaic composition, Arabic Lattice uses every available bit of space in equal assignments of positive and negative. This is an old pattern (approximately 1850) that has a contemporary look and lends itself to many color combinations, as do many "old" designs.

In the Middle Ages, characteristics of animals were used to illustrate points of moral significance and religious precepts. Unlike fables, which were meant to be instructive and to entertain, these writings were offered as truths not to be challenged on either scientific or moral grounds. Among the horses and donkeys of the real world were the dragons, sea-monsters, vipers, griffins, manticores, and the most famous of all medieval beasts—the unicorn, which has a place here in the Templates Section. In the Late Middle Ages, as medieval society developed, tournaments were arranged for knights and their horses to participate in games of battle. Playing chess gave the knights an opportunity to practise strategy for future combat and helped them while away the peacetime hours. Though the subject matter is medieval, the methods used in the *Checkmate Quilt* are as modern as possible. Everything on today's market has been utilized to make this quilt fast and easy. It is made in five sections using machine piecing and appliqué with machine quilting.

The thoroughly modern *Rhinos on Record* is made of a central design of wedges designed by paper folding and assembled by machine appliqué. A small herd of rhinos decorates the border. Each part of the design is repeated, as is the quilting, which simulates the grooves on a phonograph record. Other designs can be done by the paper-folding method for the center, and other animals can be used on the border. The entire center might make an attractive medallion for a larger quilt, with the elements of the center repeated throughout the quilt.

In areas that turn very cold, animals hibernate or sleep through the winter. They find a deep hole, cave, or similar housing, and don't come out until spring. They don't eat all winter long. In the warmer months, they eat enough to store the extra in the form of fat, to get them through the long winter night. Sleeping doesn't require nearly the amount of energy that the active life does. During the winter, humans throw a blanket or two on the bed, raise the thermostat, or put on warm clothing.

The *Snow Bunnies Wall Quilt's* bunnies are teamed up with a two-part snowflake, cut from folded cloth. Using the shadow appliqué technique makes it a fast and easy project. Whether it will be for warmth or for decoration, or a bit of both, depends on your choice of batting thickness.

Do we make quilts to keep ourselves warm? Sometimes "yes" and sometimes "no." I haven't taken a survey, but I suspect that the answer is more "no" than "yes." There is a wide range of batting available for purchase. It ranges from very thin to very thick. It would be logical to assume that if it's on the market, there is a market. I have always assumed that was so, in spite of the fact that I only see thin quilts on display at quilt shows and antique shops. This includes the contemporary ones as well as the antique. Perhaps it is that I live in a relatively warm area. Yes, it does get cool at night, but it isn't Alaska or Montana.

One day, a student of mine produced a quilt made by an ancestor. This was back in the days when many quilts were not valued by their owners and were being used for all sorts of purposes for which they were not intended. This vintage piece, with fine stitches and artistic design, had a few cigarette holes in it. The class took advantage of the opportunity to look inside and see what the filler was. It was an extremely thin cotton batting. Even if it had been used and used, would the filler have compressed to such an extent? Impossible, for excepting the results of careless smoking, the quilt was in very good condition.

I have always wondered how the makers of antique quilts had the time, energy, and artistry to make a pile of quilts sufficiently high to get them through the winter without freezing to death. Was I wrong in my notion of a spartan breed of pioneer women, laboring away without the benefit of modern machinery, electricity, and extended longevity to make these beautifully crafted masterpieces?

The answer to this mystery is that we tend to think the word "quilt" means a thickly padded bed covering. In the early days, a "quilt" simply meant any bedcover.

Think about all the thin quilts you have seen that have survived from the past. Quiltmakers of the past were a lot like us, making their special quilts to be seen, and their less decorative efforts to be used. The decorative medallion centers of *Carousel Horses* and *Armadillos Medallion Wall Quilts*, and the distinctive layouts of the *Puppy Love Wall Quilt* and the *Dairy Checkers Quilt* may make them tomorrow's showpieces.

I hope you will find the four cats on the *Kasuri Cats Pillows* as irresistible as I do. They combine Japanese fabrics, quilting, and subject matter, all of which can easily be adapted to your supplies. Kasuri fabrics are woven by hand and machine as a cottage industry in part of Japan. All of the patterns are formed by resist-dyeing both warp and weft threads and then weaving the two to make the design. This process is known as Ikat (pronounced ee-cat). These fabrics are woven for kimono and kimono-related garments and are only 14″ wide. Made of cotton, a variety of colors is used, but very dark blues predominate, due to dyeing the fabric in indigo.

Sashiko is a form of Japanese quilting that began as other quilting did, as a way to make fabrics warmer. Two layers of cloth were stitched together and the stitches were very ordinary at first. In response to a desire for more beautiful clothing, decorative patterns were adapted from nature.

The *Kasuri Cats Pillows* demonstrate one way of combining the simple with the distinctive. A simple animal shape is an effective way to show off a special fabric. Here, simple channel quilting contrasts with a more complex sashiko quilting pattern. Any quilting pattern, including the outline of a traditional or original block pattern, appliquéd or pieced, can be used to complement a special fabric in your collection.

The *Shisha Elephant Windsock*, the *Shaggy Dog Tote Bag* and the *Goldfish Soft Fabric Box* are three small projects that are easy to do, quick to make, and provocative. You'll get many inquiries from those who see them. Even a serious quiltmaker enjoys a diversion now and then. There is a satisfaction in completing a project quickly and using it on the same day.

PAT'S PET SHOP

Pat's Pet Shop Quilt

30" × 54"

MATERIALS

Light Fabric—3½ yards (includes backing)
Dark Fabric—assorted colors totalling 1 yard
Quilting Thread
Press-on Letters or a Letter Stencil—letters 2" to 3"
  high
Embroidery Floss—to contrast with appliqué color
Quilt Batting—31" × 55"

DIRECTIONS

1. Prepare templates for the lizard, fishbowl and fish, cat #1 as is, cat #2 reduced 50% at your copy shop, cat #3 reduced 50%, and the Airedale.
2. Mark and cut out animals from the assorted dark fabrics. Use the drawing as a guide.

Illus. 77. Pat's Pet Shop Quilt *design.*

3. Use a stencil to mark and cut out letters. Use the name of the recipient of the quilt. Iron-on letters can be substituted, if desired. Follow the directions on the package.
4. Cut a backing section measuring 31" × 55" from light fabric.
5. Cut the background sections for the top. Cut three measuring 17" × 31", and one 7" × 3" for the top border (to contain the letters), all from the light fabric.
6. Appliqué letters and animals as shown in Illus. 77.
7. Assemble the sections to form the top.
8. Mark the quilting design as indicated on the diagram, or as desired.
9. Prepare for quilting, following instructions in the Techniques Section.
10. Quilt.
11. Trim edges and bind.

Melangerie Wall Hanging
30″ × 56″

MATERIALS

Backing Fabric—31″ × 57″
Quilt Batting—thin, 31″ × 57″
Fabric—black, brown, beige, yellow, red-orange,
  yellow-orange, bright green, magenta, light blue,
  dark blue cottons and polycottons for the top—
  ⅜ yard each.
Black Fabric—½ yard for the binding
White Scrap Fabric—for the panda
Quilting Thread—assorted colors for embroidery
  and quilting—both to match and to contrast
Dowel Rod—½″ diameter—36″ length

DIRECTIONS

1. Cut the background squares 1″ larger than indicated on the layout diagram. This allows ½″ additional for all the seams in the top.
2. Cut and stitch together the background fabric for the top section. Use the layout diagram for dimensions and angles of the triangular piece.
3. Transfer the patterns for the animals, letters, and sun face to see-through plastic sheets (or use tracing paper glued to lightweight cardboard). Seam allowances are included in the patterns. Transfer patterns for the parts to be applied on top of the main patterns. The cutting line is indicated by a closed line and the turn-under line is indicated by a broken line (the fish eye, for example). Make quilting templates for the reindeer, panda, and elephant.
4. Place on designated fabric, mark and cut out. Cut the branches for Section A, cutting freely, or use the broken lines on the patterns for the pangolin, possum, and loris. Cut out the letters, using assorted differently colored fabrics left over from the animals and their backgrounds.
5. Assemble Section A background. Appliqué branch and loris, possum, and pangolin.
6. Appliqué the animals, sun face, and letters to their backgrounds.
7. Add embroidery, using a contrasting color of quilting thread. Stitches are indicated on the pattern as shown in Illus. 79 and Illus. 114–125.
8. Assemble Sections B and C. Complete the top by stitching one section to another, using the layout diagram as a guide.
9. Mark for quilting. The layout diagram shows quilting patterns for each section. Channel quilting (parallel lines), placed at 1″ intervals, is used for the top, bottom, and Section C. Echo quilting (following the outline of the animals and branch), is used in Section A. It is placed at ½″ intervals. Echo quilting is not usually marked, but "eyeballed." Use the quilting

Illus. 78. Melangerie Wall Hanging.

templates to mark the reindeer, panda, and elephant backgrounds.
10. Prepare for quilting.
11. Quilt.
12. Trim. Cut two binding strips ½″ longer than the short sides (30″) and two binding strips longer than the long sides (56″). Piece to make the long strips. Bind.

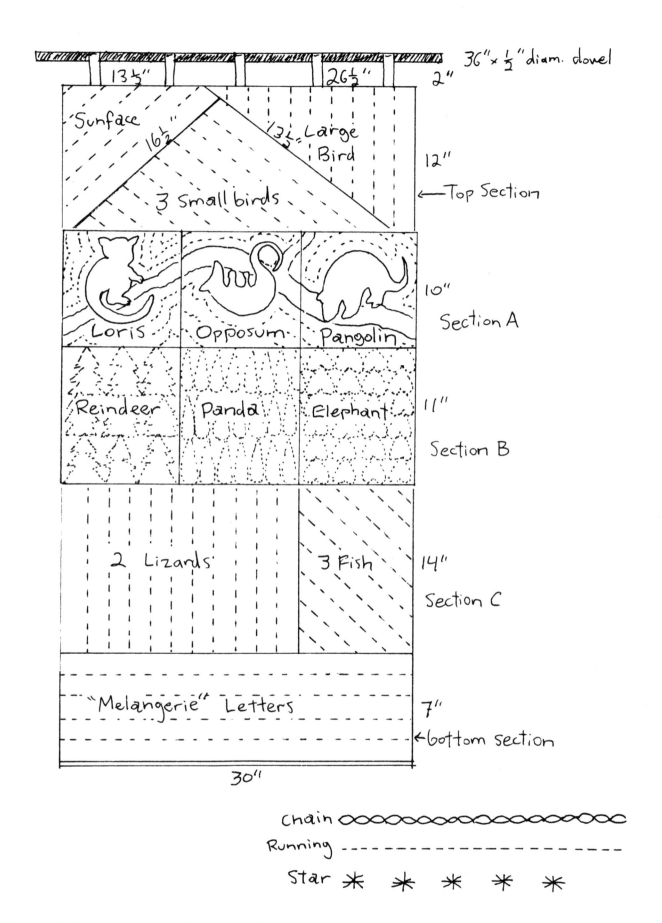

36" x ½" diam. dowel

13½" 26½" 2"

Sunface 16½" 13½" Large Bird

12"

←Top Section

3 Small birds

Loris Opposum Pangolin

10"

Section A

Reindeer Panda Elephant

11"

Section B

2 Lizards 3 Fish

14"

Section C

"Melangerie" Letters

7"

←bottom section

30"

Chain ⬡⬡⬡⬡⬡⬡⬡⬡⬡⬡

Running - - - - - - - - - - - -

Star ✳ ✳ ✳ ✳ ✳

Illus. 79. Melangerie *layout, embroidery and*
quilting diagram.

Arabian Horse Quilt
78" × 90"

MATERIALS

Backing Fabric—6 yards 45"
Quilt Batting—79" × 91"
Black Fabric—3½ yards
Red Fabric—1½ yards
White Fabric—3½ yards
Print Fabric—1 yard for the inner border
Quilting Thread—white
30°–60°–90° Triangle—to draft pattern or check
  accuracy
White Marking Pencil

DIRECTIONS

1. Prepare templates for Arabic Lattice pattern and horse by tracing and transferring to see-through plastic. (NOTE: If you wish to increase or decrease the size of the block, you can draft this block yourself. Draw a square of any size. Using the block diagram as a guide, draw a triangle of 30°–60°–90° on each side of the square. Divide the resulting square in the middle into four equal squares. Erase the superfluous lines. Use one shape each as a template.

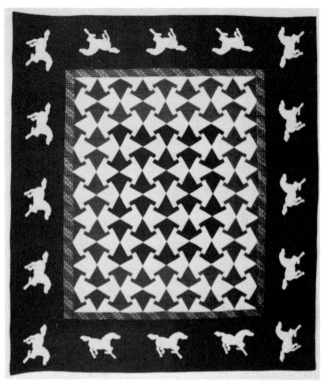

Illus. 80. Arabian Horse Quilt.

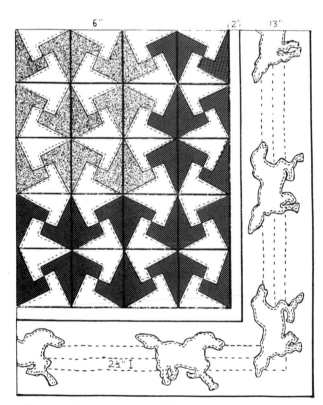

Illus. 81. Layout and quilting diagram for one-fourth of Arabian Horse Quilt.

2. Mark and cut pieces, adding a ¼" seam allowance. Make the Arabic Lattice blocks. Piece the center of the blocks first. Strip sewing, as in Illus. 83, will save time. Referring to Illus. 84, sew 2, 3, and 4 to the center. Join one side of piece 5 and then the other—do not sew into the seam allowance.

3. Cut the inner print border. Cut 2 strips measuring 3" × 49", and 2 strips measuring 3" × 65". Stitch to assembled center.

4. Cut the black border. Cut two strips measuring 14" × 53", and 2 measuring 14" × 91".

5. Use the horse template to mark the horse shapes on the black border. Find the central point on the short and long sides and position the template as shown on the diagram. Use a white pencil to mark the horse shapes, which will be done with the reverse appliqué technique.

6. Cut 16 pieces of white fabric measuring 10" × 13". Place under the marked horse shapes. Baste ⅛" outside the line marked using medium-sized even stitches. Use the reverse appliqué technique detailed in the Techniques Section. Make a starting cut of approximately ⅛" and make tiny blind stitches. Remove basting. Cut surplus fabric on the wrong side to within ½" of the stitched line.

7. Use a straightedge to mark three lines 2½" apart on the black border, as shown in the diagram. Attach border to quilt top.

8. Piece the backing fabric to measure 79" × 91". Press.

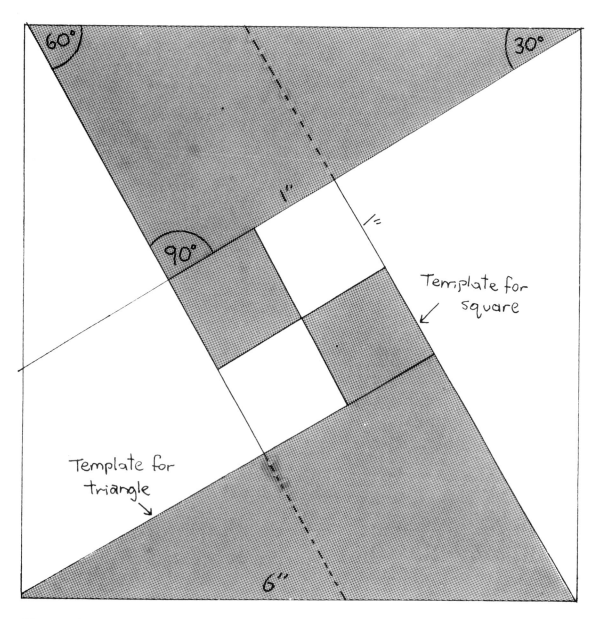

Illus. 82. Templates and diagram for "Arabic Lattice" block.

9. Prepare for quilting: Place the backing fabric right side down, batting on backing, top on batting. Center and smooth out wrinkles. Pin and/or baste at 4″ intervals horizontally and vertically from the center out.
10. Outline quilt, by hand, around each piece of the Arabic Lattice blocks and the horse shapes, and quilt along the lines marked on the border.
11. Trim the backing and batting to same size as top. Bind edges.

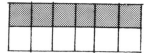

Illus. 83. Use strip-piecing techniques.

Illus. 84. Order of assembly for blocks.

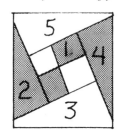

Checkmate Quilt

82″ × 108″

MATERIALS

Black Cotton Fabric—4½ yards
*Red-Purple Fabric—2½ yards (no piecing for the
    long narrow borders)*
*Fabric—blue, aqua, grey, pink, red, purple, tan,
    brown—⅝ yard each*
Backing Fabric—7 yards
Quilt Batting—bonded synthetic, 84″ × 110″
*Sewing Thread—to match appliqué colors—blue,
    aqua, grey, red, purple, red-purple, pink*
*Sewing Thread—black plus a medium color to
    piece the chessboard sections*
Featherweight Iron-on Interfacing—6 yards
Tear-away Paper—6 yards
Glue Stick
*Sewing Machine Attachments for a Zigzag
    Machine*
Open-Toe Foot
Walking Foot
Scissors
Rotary Cutter with Mat

DIRECTIONS

1. Prewash all fabrics in warm water. Iron if necessary.
2. Prepare the chessboard sections: Use the rotary cutter with self-healing mat to save time. Cut five strips from each of the colored fabrics, measuring 3½″ × width of the fabric.
3. Stitch six strips together, using a ¼″ seam allowance. Vary the placement of colors as much as possible. Cut these strips into 3½″ strips, perpendicular to the seam lines.
4. Assemble the side chessboard sections by stitching 24 rows of six colors, varying the color arrangement. Because of random planning there may be occasional places having the same colors next to each other.
5. Assemble the central chessboard by stitching eight rows of eight squares.
6. Prepare the appliqué sections; make templates of all of the chess pieces. Trace to see-through plastic or lightweight cardboard. Thick dark lines indicate that a channel should be cut to mark the interior lines.
7. Iron interfacing onto the back of the fabrics before marking and cutting out the appliqué shapes.
8. Cut the background sections from the black fabric:
    Four 90°–45°–45° Triangles—25″ × 18″ × 18″
    Two Rectangles—16″ × 35″
    Two Rectangles—16″ × 109″
9. Arrange the chess pieces as indicated in the diagram and photograph. Machine-appliqué, using a layer of tear-away paper under the area to be worked. Use a glue stick or pins to hold appliqué in place. In the large sections, basting may be helpful to secure the appliqués and keep them from shifting as you work. Stitch the outside edges and interior lines. Tear away paper.
10. Assemble the sections. Cut narrow strips from the red-purple fabric:
    Two strips—3½″ × 109″
    Two strips—3½″ × 73″
    Two strips—3½″ × 35″
11. Using the diagram, attach the appropriate-length strips to each section. Attach triangles to chessboard center, then short strips, then small appliqué panels, then side strips, in order to complete the sections. Do not sew sections together yet.
12. Prepare to machine-quilt the five sections. Cut the following backing pieces and batting:
    Two Rectangles—20″ × 110″
    Two Rectangles—23″ × 74″
    One Rectangle—36″ × 74″
13. For each section, place backing fabric right side down, with batting on top. Center and smooth out any folds or wrinkles. Pin and baste, from the middle out, at 4–6″ intervals lengthwise and widthwise.
14. Mark for quilting as indicated on the diagram. Except for outlining the appliqué shapes, all quilting is done in straight lines. Use a light or dark pencil to mark the lines, which bisect the corners of the colored squares. The channel quilting (parallel lines) is placed along the top, bottom, and center sections at 1½″ intervals.
15. Using a walking-foot attachment, the medium-colored thread on the chessboard sections, and the black thread on the appliqué sections, machine-quilt with a long stitch. I use the longest setting possible. Outline the appliqué shapes first. Next, stitch the lines. No quilting is done on the border strips.
16. Assemble the sections; attach the side sections to the center. Place right sides together on the quilt top. Pin, stitch and finger-press the seams open. Trim batting so that it does not overlap. If desired, hand-stitch the batting sections. This will prevent shifting when the quilt is washed. Turn project to the back, fold in the seam allowance on one side and blind-stitch. Attach the end sections in the same way.
17. Bind the quilt with straight strips, cut 1½″ × 109″ and 1½″ × 83″, cut two each in the same color used on the edge (red-purple).

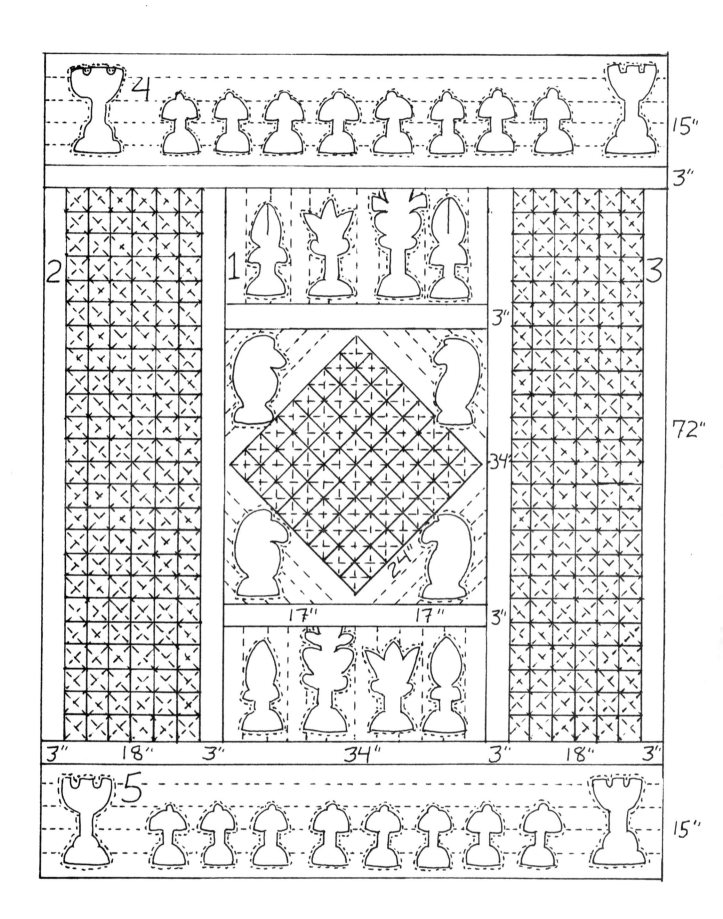

Illus. 85. Layout and quilting diagram for Checkmate.

Illus. 86. Dairy Checkers Quilt.

Dairy Checkers Quilt
47″ × 56″

MATERIALS

Dark Fabric—4 yards—includes backing and outer border
Dark and Light Fabrics—1 yard each for the checkerboard, cows, and their spots
Print Fabric—2½ yards for the black background and inner border strips
Quilt Batting—48″ × 57″

DIRECTIONS

1. Prepare templates for the cow and spots.
2. Mark and cut out six cows and six sets of spots.
3. From the print fabric, cut six background squares measuring 13″ × 16″, two strips measuring 40″ × 3″, and two strips measuring 53″ × 3″ for the inner border.
4. Place spots on the cows, and place cows on the background rectangles. Appliqué in place.

5. Cut 14 strips each from the dark and light fabrics. They should measure 2″ × the width of the fabric purchased. Depending on the width purchased, cut enough strips to make all the checkerboard sections shown on the drawing through strip piecing. Stitch a dark strip to a light. Mark again in 2″ intervals and cut and restitch to make the checkerboard strips. Make nine strips 12½″ long and four strips 39½″ long.
6. Attach checkerboard sections to the 12″ sides of the cow blocks. Complete three rows of two cows and checkerboard strips.
7. Attach long checkerboard strips as indicated on the drawing.
8. Attach the inner print border.
9. Cut the outer border strips. Cut two measuring 3″ × 44″ and two measuring 3″ × 57″.
10. Mark for quilting.
11. Quilt around the cows and along the checkerboard strips, or in any desired quilting pattern.
12. Trim and bind.

Illus. 87. Bear's Paw Wall Quilt.

Bear's Paw Wall Quilt
32″ × 44″

MATERIALS

Light Solid Fabric—¼ yard
Dark Solid Fabric—1¼ yards
Print Fabric—2¼ yards—(includes backing fabric)
Quilting Thread—dark or light to match or
  contrast
Quilt Batting—33″ × 45″

DIRECTIONS

1. Prepare bear template. Reduce one-third at your copy shop to make a template for the border bear. Prepare triangle template.
2. Cut four large-print bears, and eight small-print bears. Cut sixteen dark triangles, sixteen print triangles, six print squares, one dark square, and four print rectangular sections (two squares together). Also, cut two strips measuring 9″ × 29″ and two strips measuring 3″ × 45″ for the border, and four 8½″ background squares from the dark fabric.
3. Piece the top row by row as shown in Illus. 87. Assemble the triangles to make squares, the rectangles to make rows, and the rows and borders to make the top.
4. Appliqué bears to borders (this can be done before adding to the top, if desired).
5. Appliqué bears to center (over seams, if desired, as shown on the drawing).
6. Prepare for quilting.
7. Quilt around the bears and geometric shapes, or in any desired pattern.
8. Trim edges. Bind.

Armadillos Medallion Wall Quilt

31" × 31"

MATERIALS

*Print Fabrics—4 or more different prints to make
a total of 1–1½ yards*
Backing Fabric—1 yard
*Light Solid Fabric—23" × 23", to make the back-
ground for the medallion*
Quilt Batting—32" square
Quilting Thread

DIRECTIONS

1. Prepare templates for the armadillos, wedge inserts, and a right triangle (90°–45°–45°) measuring
11" × 11" × 15½".

2. From one of the print fabrics mark and cut four
armadillos.

3. From all of the print fabrics, cut 1½" strips ×
width of the fabric. Stitch together and mark and cut
eight right-angle triangles measuring 15½" × 11" ×
11", allowing ¼" for a seam allowance (Illus. 89).

4. Mark and cut eight wedge inserts using Illus. 88 as
a guide.

5. Cut a 1" strip, 20" long, from the same print used
for armadillos. Stitch between two wedge inserts.

6. Appliqué inserts to armadillos.

7. Position armadillos on the solid background
square. Use the diagram as a guide.

8. Assemble the triangular corners and attach to center.

9. Mark top for quilting as shown on diagram or in
any desired pattern. Use large platters or a beam
compass—a special compass used for making large
circles—to mark circles.

10. Prepare for quilting. Quilt.

11. Trim and bind.

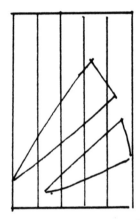

Illus. 88. Place wedge inserts on pieced strips at an angle as shown.

Illus. 89. Make corner triangles of pieced strips as shown.

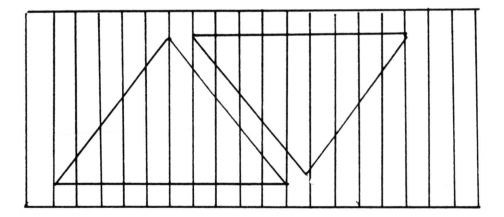

Illus. 90. Layout and quilting guide for Armadillos Medallion Wall Quilt.

Illus. 91. Rhinos on Record.

Rhinos on Record Wall Quilt

34"-diameter wall quilt mounted on an optional 36"-square frame

MATERIALS

Black Fabric—1 yard
Light Grey Fabric—½ yard
Fabric—bright red, white, grey pindot, dark grey, grey print, black pindot—¼ yard each
Featherweight Fusible Interfacing—white, cut to a 19" circle
Tear-away Paper—cut to a 19" circle
Quilting Thread—black and red—1 spool each
Protractor
Flexible Curve—purchase from an engineering supplier
Sewing Thread—grey—2 spools

MATERIALS FOR OPTIONAL FRAME

Red Flannel—1½ yards
Stretcher Bars—Four 36"-length bars
Thumbtacks—2 cards
Staple Gun—staples

DIRECTIONS

1. Cut a 34" circle from the black fabric. Reserve the remainder for the bias binding.
2. Fold the fusible interfacing circle in half and divide the halves into thirds, using a protractor to ensure equal sections.

3. Trace the rhino pattern onto see-through plastic and cut out. Trace the two wedges. Transfer the wedge design onto the nonsticky side of the fusible interfacing. Alternate the wedge patterns. Number each section. Make a photocopy of the wedge patterns to use as a placement guide. Cut the sections apart on each wedge. Each numbered piece is to be fused to a different fabric (wrong side). Fuse fabrics and cut out.

5. Arrange the pieces as indicated in placement guide, edges touching. Pin and/or glue in place. Basting is not necessary, but will aid in securing the pieces on the "record label," and is a good preparation for the machine-appliquéing process. Place tear-away paper under the center. Pin in place from the top.

6. Using the grey sewing thread, machine-appliqué with a wide satin stitch, catching both edges of adjacent pieces. Repeat if additional coverage is desired.

7. Cut a 1½" circle from the black fabric and hand-appliqué to the center of the label.

8. Place the rhinos at even intervals. Place the feet on the label as indicated on the photo. Pin and/or baste in place. Hand-appliqué with a blind stitch.

9. Mark the interior lines on the rhinos and the rings on the record border. I used a flexible curve, purchased from an engineering supplier. Start marking from the outside edge of the label.

10. Quilt on the lines. Embroider the rhinos' eyes using the quilting thread. Quilt the edges of each section of the record label. I used red quilting thread on the label, and black for the rest.

11. Make a bias strip (cut on the diagonal at a 45° angle to the grain of the fabric) from the remainder of the black polished cotton, measuring 2½" × 108". Mark the strips 1½" by the longest bias length and piece to make the length needed. Bind. The wall quilt can be used without a frame.

12. Or, make and cover the frame, if desired; fit the stretcher bars together to make the frame. Tap corners in place with a hammer. Staple corners for additional stability. Place the red flannel down on a table or floor and place the frame on top. Using the tacks, pull and tack the middle of each side of the frame, working outward. Remove and add tacks while tightening. When the flannel is taut, use the staple gun; then remove the tacks. At the corners, pull the fabric to the middle, tack and staple. Cut away excess fabric. Pin the record circle to the middle of the flannel-covered frame. Velcro pieces can be sewn to both the quilted record and the flannel board, or glued, if desired.

Illus. 92. Snow Bunnies Wall Quilt.

Snow Bunnies Wall Quilt
45″ × 45″

MATERIALS

Backing Fabric—46″ × 46″
Medium-Blue Background Fabric—1⅛ yards to make the central square
White Sheer Fabric—1⅛ yards to cover the central square
Ice-Blue Fabric—⅝ yard for the blue snowflake
White Fabric—¼ yard for the inner border
Blue Fabric—⅝ yard for the outer border
Pellon Fleece (compressed batting)—1 yard for the white snowflake and bunnies
Quilt Batting—46″ × 46″
Iron-on Featherweight Interfacing—20″ square
White Quilting Thread
Washable Glue Stick

DIRECTIONS

1. Prepare templates for the bunny and snowflakes #1 and #2.
2. Cut:
   Four strips measuring 1½″ × 38″ from the white fabric
   Two strips measuring 5″ × 39″ and two measuring 5″ × 46″ from the blue outer-border fabric
   One 37″ square from the blue background
   One 37″ square from the white sheer fabric
3. Follow the folding procedure for the snowflake templates and make full patterns using a paper bag.
4. Fuse the iron-on interfacing to the wrong side of the ice-blue fabric.
5. Cut the #1 snowflake and six bunnies from the fleece (which needs no basting or other such stabilization). Cut the #2 snowflake from the ice-blue fabric.
6. To divide the blue background fabric into six equal wedges, use the folding procedure used to make the snowflakes. Press to crease, and open.
7. Using the just-created, ironed-in lines as a placement guide for the position of the snowflakes, first position the white snowflake, and then the ice-blue snowflake on top of the white snowflake. Arrange the bunnies as shown in Illus. 92.
8. Glue the bunnies and snowflakes in place. Cover with the sheer fabric. Baste, if desired, to anchor the design, or use safety pins.
9. Attach the white inner border and then the blue outer border. Press all seams and press to remove fold lines.
10. Prepare to quilt: place backing fabric right side down, put batting on backing, and the top on the batting. Pin and baste at 4″ intervals lengthwise and widthwise, working out from the middle.
11. Outline the outside edge of the bunnies and snowflakes with hand quilting.
12. To develop a quilting pattern on the background, draw lines from the outside central points of the snowflakes to the edge of the background. If the quilt will be used and washed frequently, add enough lines so that there will be some quilting stitches every four to six inches on the width and length.
13. Trim the outside edges of the backing and batting even with the top. Fold in the seam allowance and hand-stitch closed.

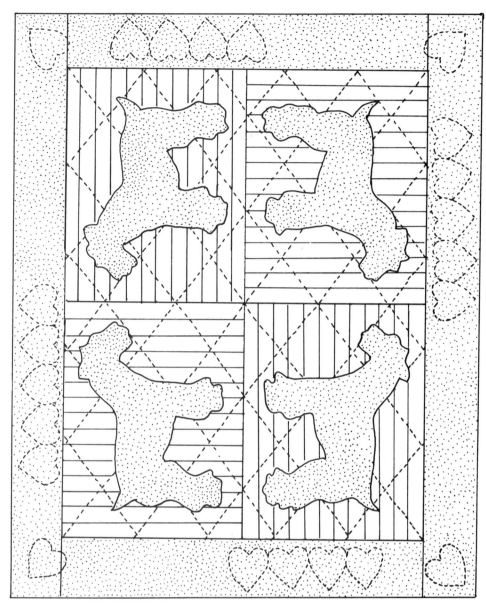

Illus. 93. Layout and quilting diagram for Puppy Love Wall Quilt.

Puppy Love Wall Quilt
36″ × 42″

MATERIALS

*Print Fabric—2½ yards—includes backing and
    border
Solid Fabrics—assorted colors—1½ to 2 yards
Quilt Batting—37″ × 43″
Quilting Thread—to match or contrast*

DIRECTIONS

1. Prepare templates for Airedale terrier and heart
quilting pattern.

2. From the print fabric, mark and cut four Airedales, two strips 7″ × 25″, and two strips 7″ × 43″.
3. Assemble four background blocks by cutting 1½″
strips from the assorted solid fabrics. Stitch together
to make 13″ × 16″ background.
4. Appliqué Airedales to background blocks.
5. Assemble the top as indicated in Illus. 93.
6. Attach the borders.
7. Mark for quilting as indicated, or as desired.
8. Prepare for quilting. Quilt.
9. Trim and bind.

Fisheating Creek *by Jean Eitel. Photo by artist.*

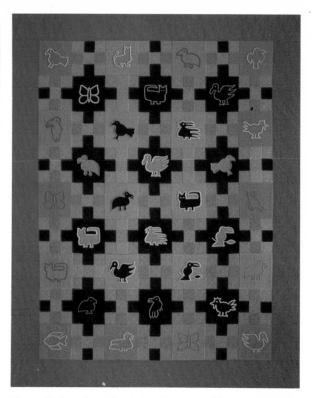

Kuna Echos *by Charlotte Patera. Photo by artist.*

At Night *by Michael Cummings. Photo by artist.*

Guardians of Fiery Mountain #3 © *by Nancy Erickson. Photo by artist.*

Above: Snow Bunnies Wall Quilt *by Charlyne Stewart.*

Below: Checkmate Quilt *by Charlyne Stewart.*

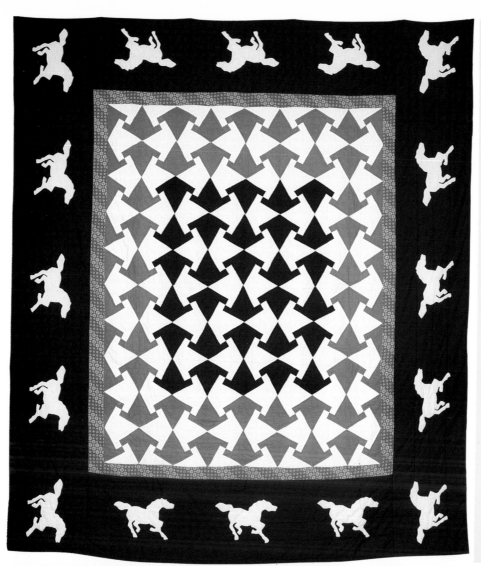

Clockwise from top: Arabian Horse Quilt; Goldfish Soft Fabric Box; *and* Rhinos on Record Wall Quilt, *all by Charlyne Stewart.*

Illus. 94. Layout diagram for Carousel Horses Wall Quilt.

Carousel Horses Wall Quilt

30″ × 36″

MATERIALS

Print Fabric—2 yards (includes backing and border)
Light Fabric—1¼ yards
Dark Solid Fabric—½ yard
Quilt Batting—31″ × 37″
Quilting Thread

DIRECTIONS

1. Prepare template for horse and all triangles.
2. Make a right angle (90°–45°–45°) triangle measuring 12″ × 12″ × 17″. Place triangle B at top edges. Draw a line. Cut off top and use the remainder as triangle A to make the background. Triangles B, C and D are in the Templates Section.
3. From the light fabric, mark and cut: eight triangle Bs, 96 triangle Cs, and 112 triangle Ds.

4. Piece the large triangular central section by piecing triangle B to triangle A (see Step 2). Assemble the central section and appliqué the carousel horses.
5. Assemble the rows of triangle C's and D's as indicated in Illus. 94.
6. Mark for quilting in any desired pattern, or outline the horses and triangles.
7. Prepare for quilting.
8. Quilt.
9. Trim and bind.

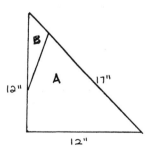

Illus. 95. Layout diagram for triangles A and B.

Illus. 96. The four Kasuri Cat Pillows.

Kasuri Cat Pillows

16″ × 16″

MATERIALS

Kasuri Fabric—1 yard of 14″-wide fabric for each
    pillow (the sample is made of two fabrics, ½ yard
    each) **or** substitute any dark-blue cotton that is
    36″- to 45″-wide—½ yard
Light-Blue Cotton Fabric—15″ square for each
    pillow
Backing Fabric—16″ square for each pillow
Lightweight Batting—16″ square for each pillow
Red Fabric Scraps
Quilting Thread—navy and white—1 spool each
Pillow Forms—16″ square, or make your own pillow
    form from:
    Quilt Batting—heavy-bonded, ½ yard
    Polyester Fibrefill Stuffing—½ lb.
    Dressmaker's Carbon
    Red Ballpoint Pen

DIRECTIONS

1. Trace the cat patterns and quilting patterns from
the book.
2. Mark cat(s) and cut out from the Kasuri or dark-
blue fabric. Seam allowances are included in each cat
pattern. Mark and cut the ball from the red scrap
fabric.
3. To transfer the quilting patterns to the pillow top,
place the light-blue square right side up. Place the
waxy side of the dressmaker's carbon on the square.
Place the quilting pattern on top of the carbon, posi-
tioning it to correspond with the photos of the pillows. Pin in place on the outside edges. Use a red
ballpoint pen to transfer the quilting pattern. It will
help you to see which lines you have transferred and
which you have not. Mark the remainder of the quilting lines; the channel (or parallel) lines are placed at
1″ intervals with a #2 pencil. Marking can also be
done after the appliquéing is completed.
4. Pin the cat and ball to the background square.
Baste and appliqué.
5. Prepare the quilt: Place the backing square right
side down, the batting on the backing square, and
the cat appliqué pillow top on the batting. Center.
Pin and/or baste in 4″ intervals horizontally and vertically.
6. Use the navy quilting thread to outline the cat,
ball and sashiko (transferred quilting pattern). Use
white thread to quilt the parallel lines (channel quilting).
7. To make the back and border for the pillow top, cut
four strips measuring 2″ × 18″. Stitch to pillow top
center. Trim any excess.
8. Cut square for the back measuring 17″ square.
(The strips and backing can be cut from the same
patterned fabric as the cat appliqué, or use a second
patterned fabric.)
9. If you are making your own pillow form, it should
be the same size or slightly larger than the pillow
cover. Fold the thick batting in half and stitch on two
sides, after trimming to make it correspond to the
dimensions of the pillow top. Finger-press the batting as it goes under the presser foot to prevent it
from catching. Turn right side out. Stuff with
fibrefill. Fold in the seam allowance on the remaining
side and hand-stitch closed.
10. Insert pillow form into cover. Fold in seam allowance on the opening and hand-stitch closed.

Shisha Embroidered Elephant Windsock

MATERIALS

Light Solid Fabric—21" × 32"
Dark Solid Fabric—1 yard
Medium Fabric—⅛ yard. NOTE: For outdoor use, waterproof and colorfast synthetic fabric such as ripstop nylon is best
Metal Ring—10" diameter (purchase from a hobby shop)
Grosgrain Ribbon—3 yards of ⅜"-width ribbon
Mirror Pieces (Shisha)—⅝" to 1" diameter—44 Mirrors, or substitute 88 dime-sized circles cut from heavy-duty aluminum pan foil. Place one circle on top of another to make a double thickness.
Perle Cotton—2 skeins. NOTE: For outdoor use, substitute synthetic thread or floss
Bells—4 brass bells or jingle bells

DIRECTIONS

1. Prepare template for elephant, showing mirror embroidery placement, and templates for flap, ear, and headpiece/saddle.

2. From the dark fabric, mark and cut: two elephants, eight flaps, and four strips measuring 3" × 32" for the top and bottom border strips and facings. From the medium-colored fabric, mark and cut two ears and two headpieces.

3. Fold under ½" seam allowance on the short sides of the background light fabric rectangle. Press to wrong side. Find center points by pressing remainder in half lengthwise and widthwise (Illus. 98). Press.

4. Place one elephant in each section, centered.

5. Place ears and headpieces on elephant, and appliqué to background. Attach mirrors. See the Techniques Section for details.

6. Place a dark strip on the top and bottom of the background rectangle, right sides together. Stitch in place. Press.

7. Face all flaps right sides together. Stitch along the seam line of the curved sides. Turn right sides out and press.

8. Pin the four faced flaps to the edge of the bottom strip (Illus. 99). Stitch in place.

9. Fold the rectangle in half lengthwise, right sides together, matching seam lines of top and bottom border strips. Stitch, using the pressed seam line as a guide.

10. Fold the remaining dark strips (facing bands) in half lengthwise to make a continuous piece. Place on top and bottom edges, right sides together. Stitch. Press. On the bottom edge, pull the flaps down.

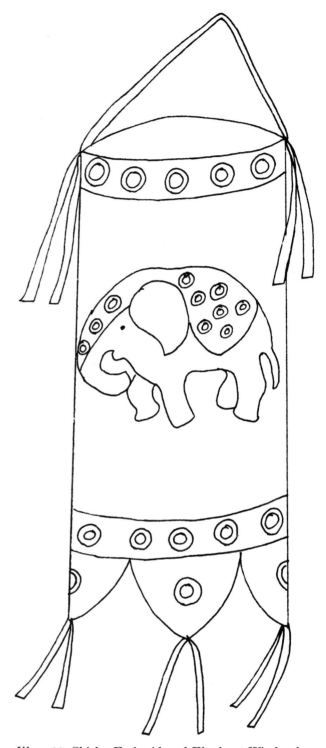

Illus. 97. Shisha Embroidered Elephant Windsock.

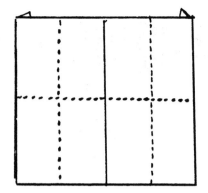

Illus. 98. Fold and press background rectangle as shown.

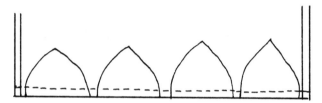

Illus. 99. Pin the four flaps to the edge of the bottom strip and stitch.

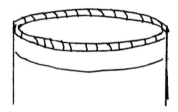

Illus. 100. Fold top facing band over metal hoop and whipstitch in place.

11. Place the metal hoop on the seam line of the top edge. Fold the facing band over it. Whip-stitch in place (Illus. 100).

12. Turn the windsock inside out. Fold in the seam allowances on the top and bottom facing bands. Hand-stitch in place. Turn to right side.

13. Cut six lengths of ribbon 14″ long and 1 length 20″ long for a hanging loop.

14. Tack long-length (20″) ribbon to seam line on opposite ends of top of ring for hanging loop. Fold six short-length (14″) ribbons in half. Tack a ribbon at midpoint to each of the four flaps. Add a bell. Tack remaining two ribbons on their midpoints to each end of the hanging loop.

Shaggy Dog Tote Bag
11″ × 16″ × 4″

MATERIALS

White Canvas—heavyweight—¾ yard
Brown Print Cotton Fabric—½ yard for the lining
Fabric Scraps—light-brown print, dark-brown print, medium-brown solid cotton (use the lining fabric as one of these)
Tear-away Paper—9″ square
Featherweight Fusible Interfacing—9″ square
Sewing Thread—brown and white—1 spool each
Embroidery Floss—red and brown—1 strand each

DIRECTIONS

1. From both the white canvas and the brown print lining fabric cut:
   Two rectangles—12″ × 16″ for the front and back
   One rectangle—5″ × 40″ for the sides/bottom
2. From the canvas only, cut two straps measuring 2″ × 25″.
3. Transfer the dog pattern from the book to the fusible interfacing; place over the pattern and trace to the nonfusible side.
4. Cut the dog pattern sections apart and fuse to the designated fabrics, on the wrong side.
5. Position the dog appliqué on the outer bag front. Pin and/or glue in place. Baste, if desired.
6. Place the tear-away paper under the area to be appliquéd. Machine-appliqué on all edges. On all the interior lines catch both edges with the stitch. Use a setting wide enough to catch adjacent edges. Embroider details on dog's face.
7. Assemble the bag: stitch the side to the front section, using a ½″ seam allowance (used throughout), clipping at the corners of the front and/or side section to turn.
8. Repeat for back outer bag section. Repeat this procedure for the lining, which is assembled separately, *except* leave a 4″ opening on one of the lining bottom-sections.
9. Make straps: Fold the canvas straps in half lengthwise and in half again to make four layers. Stitch on the edges of both sides.
10. Place the straps on the outer bag, back and front, facing down. Measuring from the center, pin 8″ apart. Stitch in place.
11. Place the lining bag over the outer bag, right sides together. Pin and stitch on the top edge, reinforcing with additional stitching where straps are placed.
12. Flip the lining to the inside of the outer bag. Pull the straps up. Lift the bottom on the lining bag. Fold in the seam allowance in the 4″ opening and hand- or machine-stitch closed. Return to the inside bottom of the outer bag. Press the top edge.

Illus. 101. Shaggy Dog Tote Bag.

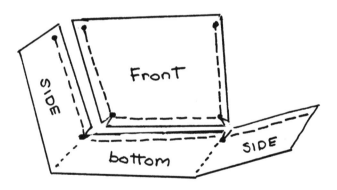

Illus. 102. Assemble the canvas bag as shown.

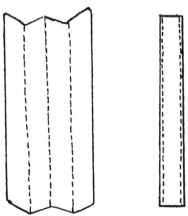

Illus. 103. Fold and stitch carrying straps as shown.

Illus. 104. Pin ends of straps 8" apart.

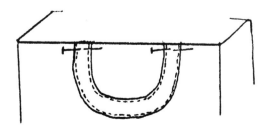

Illus. 105. Goldfish Soft Fabric Box.

Goldfish Soft Fabric Box
9″ × 5″ × 2½″

MATERIALS

Metallic Fabric—gold stretch synthetic—¼ yard
Unbleached Muslin—6″ × 10″ rectangle
Black Cotton Fabric—10″ × 6″ rectangle for box-
  top background
Quilt Batting—thick, ¼ yard
Illustration Board—½ board
Polyester fibrefill stuffing—⅛ lb
Yarn—thick, white—1 strand
Quilting Thread—gold and black—1 spool each

DIRECTIONS

1. From the cardboard, cut:
    Two rectangles 9″ × 5″—for the top and bottom
    Two rectangles—9″ × 2½″—for the long sides
    Two rectangles—5″ × 2½″—for the short sides
2. Using one each of the cardboard shapes as tem-

plates, cut from the gold metallic fabric, allowing an additional ½″ for a seam allowance:
    Four rectangles for top backing and bottom pieces
    Four rectangles for the long sides
    Four rectangles for the short sides
3. Transfer the fish design to the unbleached muslin. Place muslin over design and trace with a #2 pencil or use dressmaker's carbon.
4. Pin fish design on muslin, face up, to the wrong side of one of the large gold metallic rectangles. Quilt on all lines of the fish design, using black quilting thread.
5. To raise the fish design, carefully lift the muslin layer on each compartment. Use a pin to separate the layers. Make a tiny cut. Use a small embroidery scissors or crochet hook to stuff a small amount of the fibrefill into each compartment, guiding it into the corners. To raise the tiny eye area, use a needle threaded with thick yarn.
6. Close each cut with a whipped stitch, shown in Illus. 107.
7. After completing the raising of the fish design, cut

right side ← Batt covered cardboard =

Illus. 106. Insert batting-covered cardboard into right-side-out fabric rectangle, fold in seam allowance and stitch open end closed.

Illus. 107. Assemble box as shown at right. View of wrong side shows how to pad the fish design.

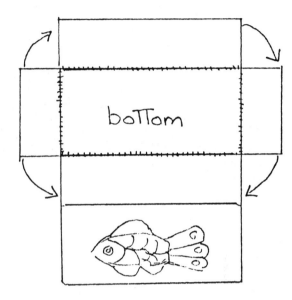

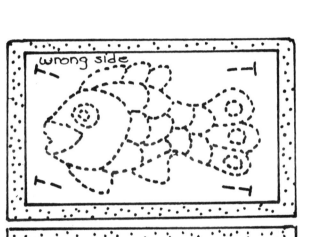

wrong side

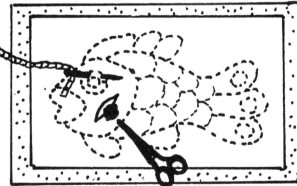

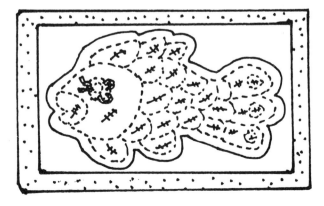

it from its rectangular background to emphasize the fish shape, allowing an additional ¼" outside the outline for a turn-under allowance.

8. To make the box top, baste the goldfish to the 10″ × 6″ black rectangle. Appliqué with the gold-colored quilting thread. Face it to the 10″ × 6″ gold rectangle, right sides together. Stitch along three sides, leaving a long side open (one parallel to the back of the fish design) for inserting similar-shaped cardboard. Trim at corners. Turn right side out.

9. Follow the same procedure for the box sides by stitching matching fabric rectangles together on three sides, leaving a short side open for inserting the matching-size cardboard shape.

10. Wrap thick batting over each cardboard shape, trimming to size. Tack in place over the cardboard. Insert it into the fabric unit, bending the cardboard, if necessary. Fold in the seam allowance and stitch closed.

11. Assemble box and stitch together. Attach cover to one of the long sides.

Part Four: Templates

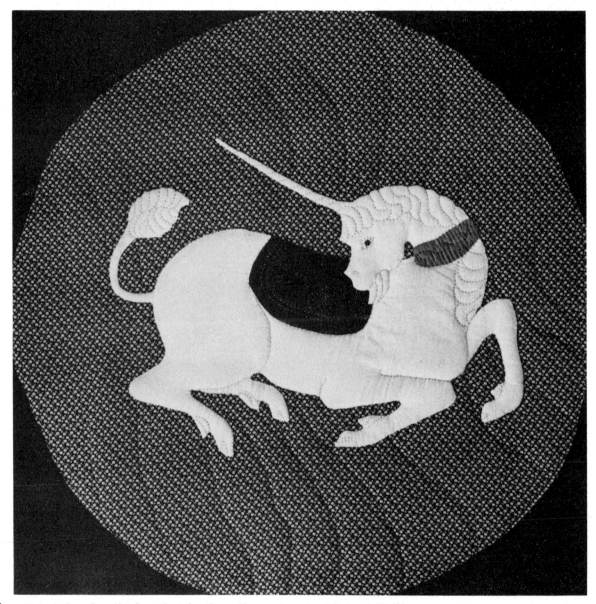

Illus. 108. A hand-quilted project by the author. Photo by Michael Heilig.

Illus. 109. Unicorn.

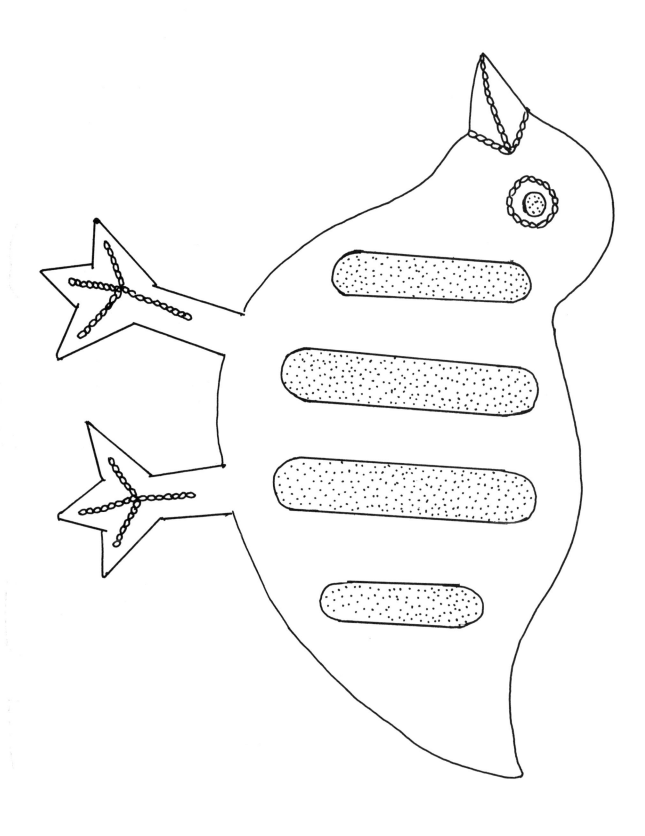

Illus. 110. Mola bird.

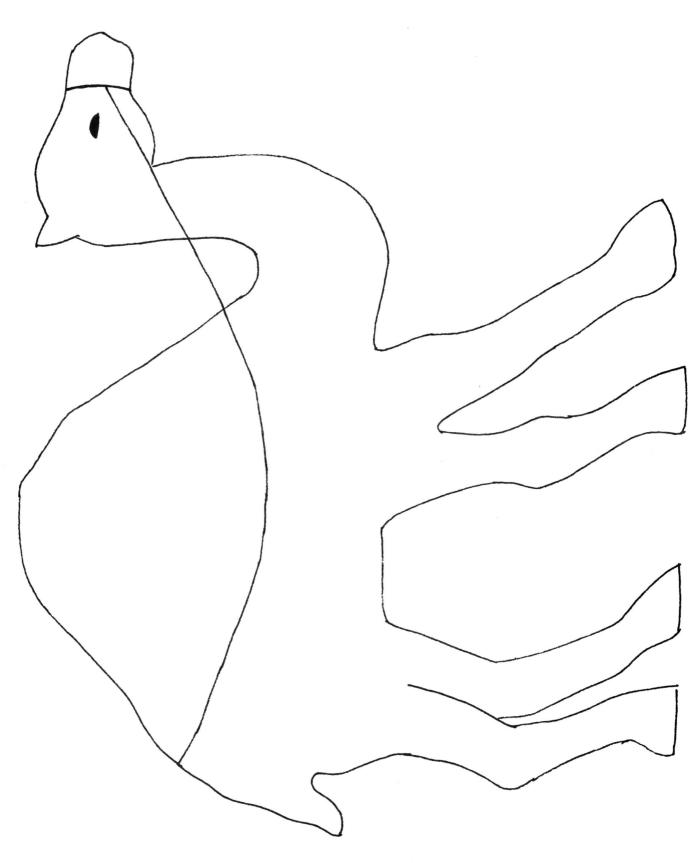

Illus. 111. Camel.

Illus. 112. Monkey.

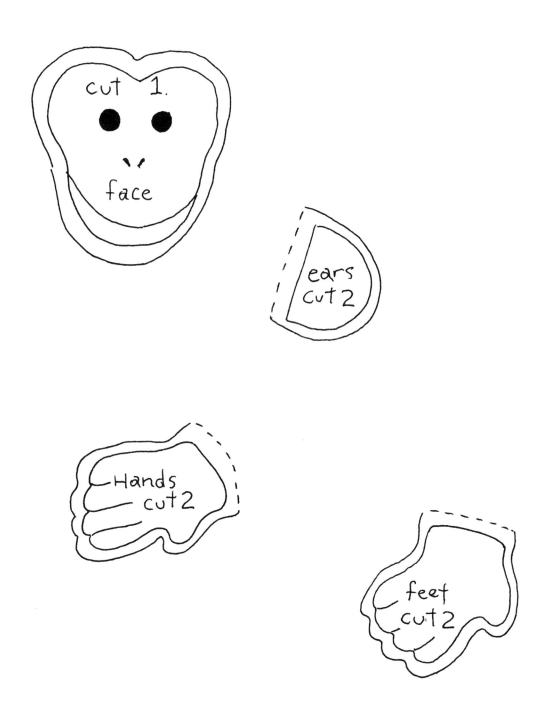

Illus. 113. Face, ears, hands and feet for monkey.

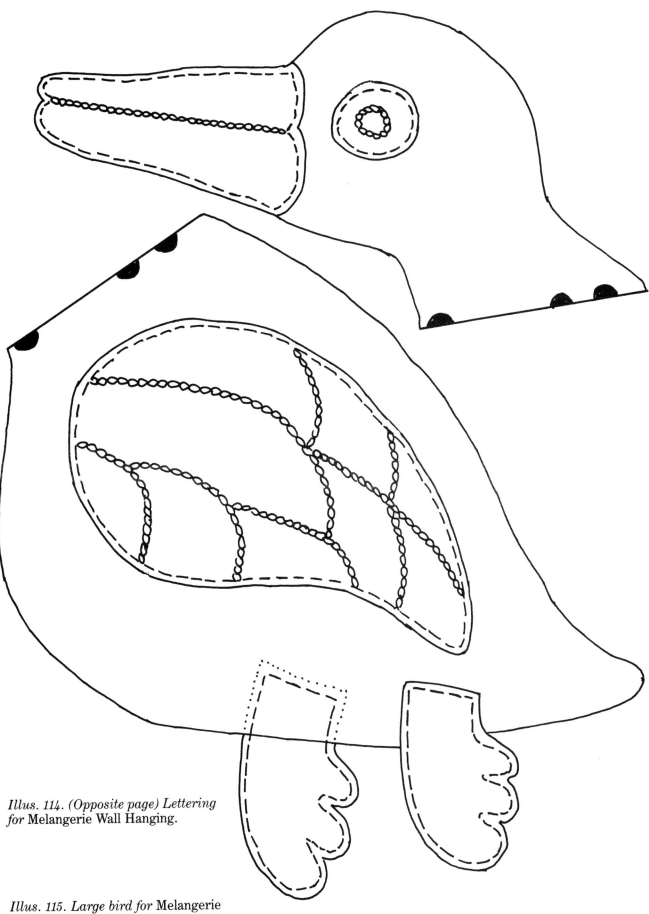

Illus. 114. (Opposite page) Lettering for Melangerie Wall Hanging.

Illus. 115. Large bird for Melangerie Wall Hanging.

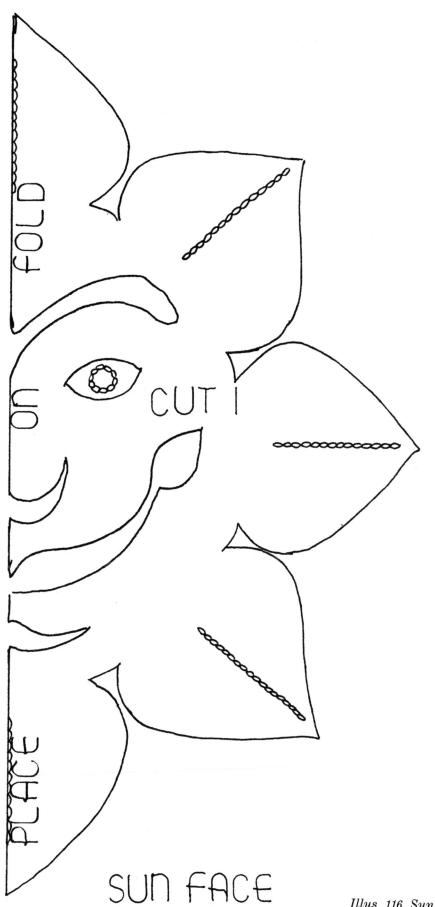

FOLD

ON

PLACE

CUT I

SUN FACE

Illus. 116. Sun face for **Melangerie Wall Hanging.**

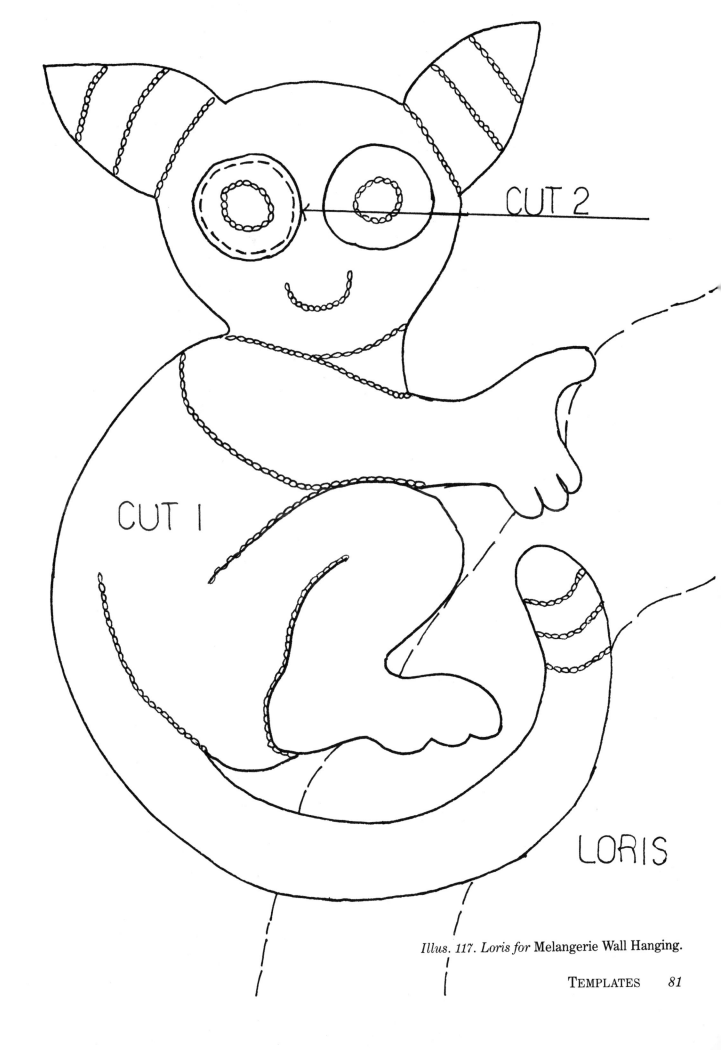

CUT 2

CUT I

LORIS

Illus. 117. Loris for Melangerie Wall Hanging.

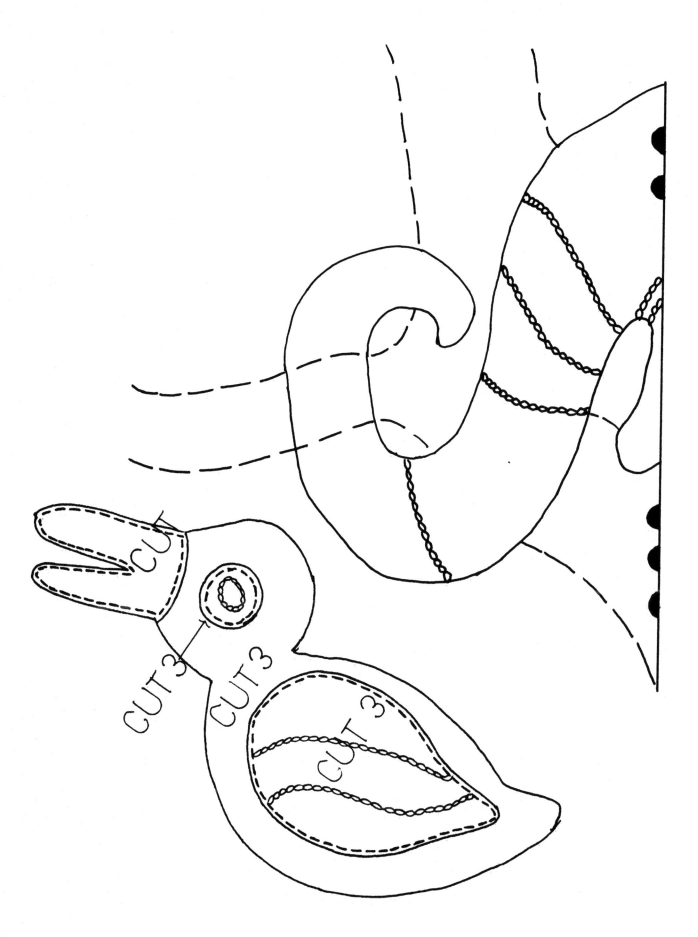

Illus. 118. Small bird for Melangerie Wall Hanging.

The following CUT labels appear within the illustration: CUT, CUT 3, CUT 3, CUT 3, CUT 3.

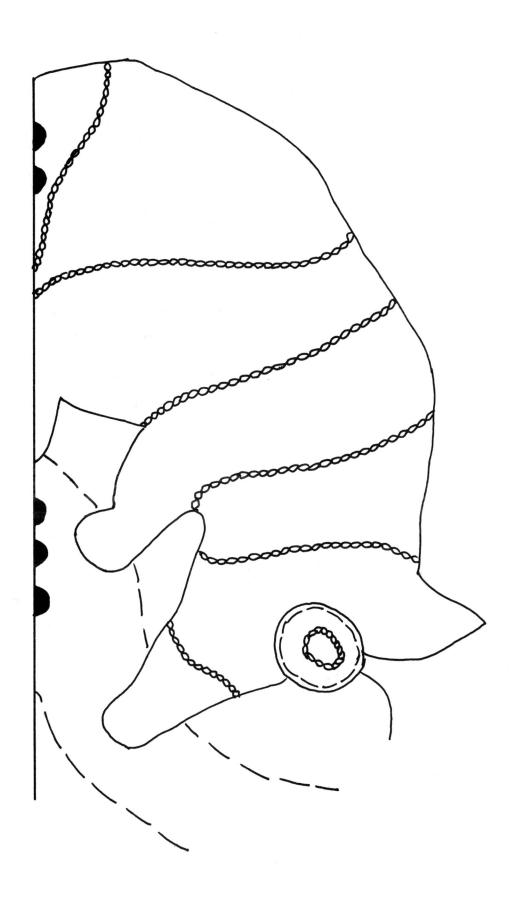

Illus. 119. Possum for Melangerie Wall Hanging.

Illus. 120. Quilting templates for Melangerie Wall Hanging: *leaf, heart, and tree.*

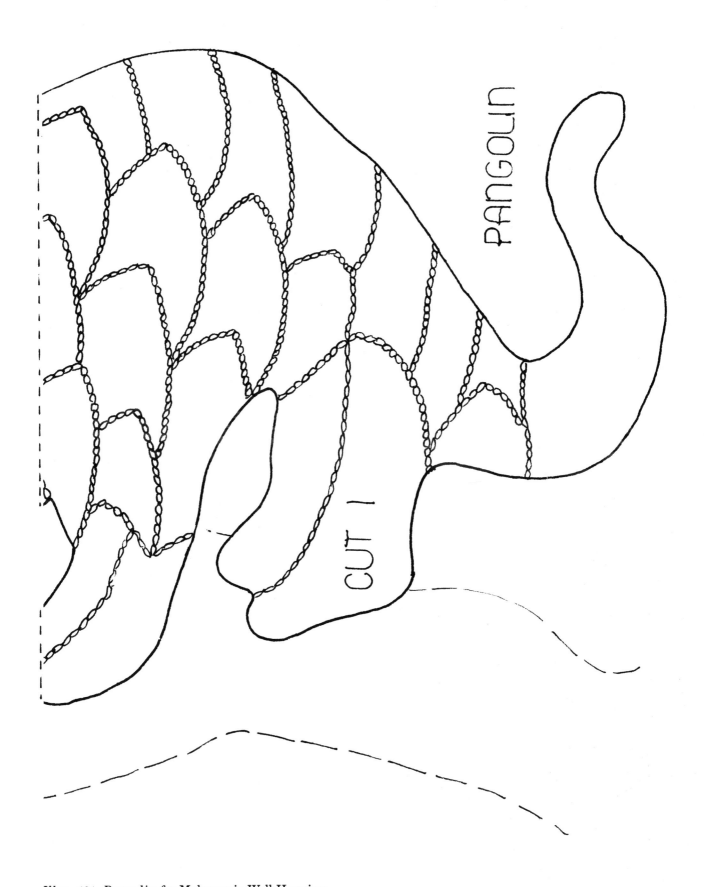

Illus. 121. Pangolin for Melangerie Wall Hanging.

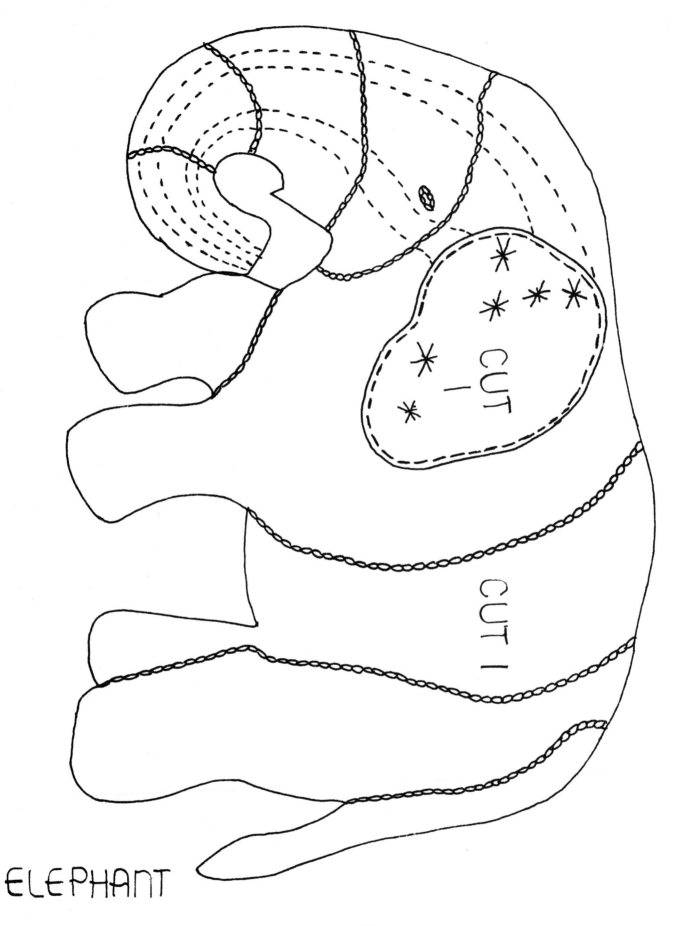

CUT
1

CUT 1

ELEPHANT

Illus. 122. Elephant for Melangerie Wall Hanging.

PANDA

Illus. 123. Panda for Melangerie Wall Hanging.

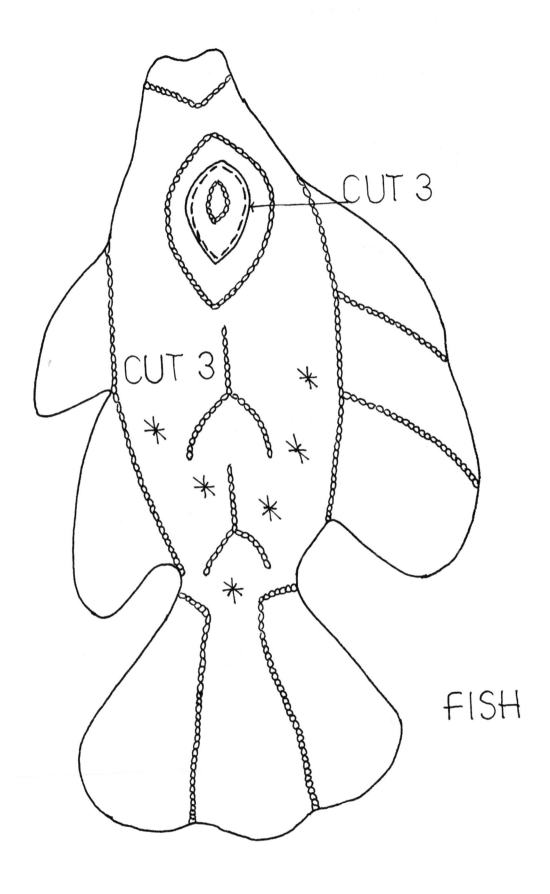

CUT 3

CUT 3

FISH

Illus. 124. Fish for Melangerie Wall Hanging.

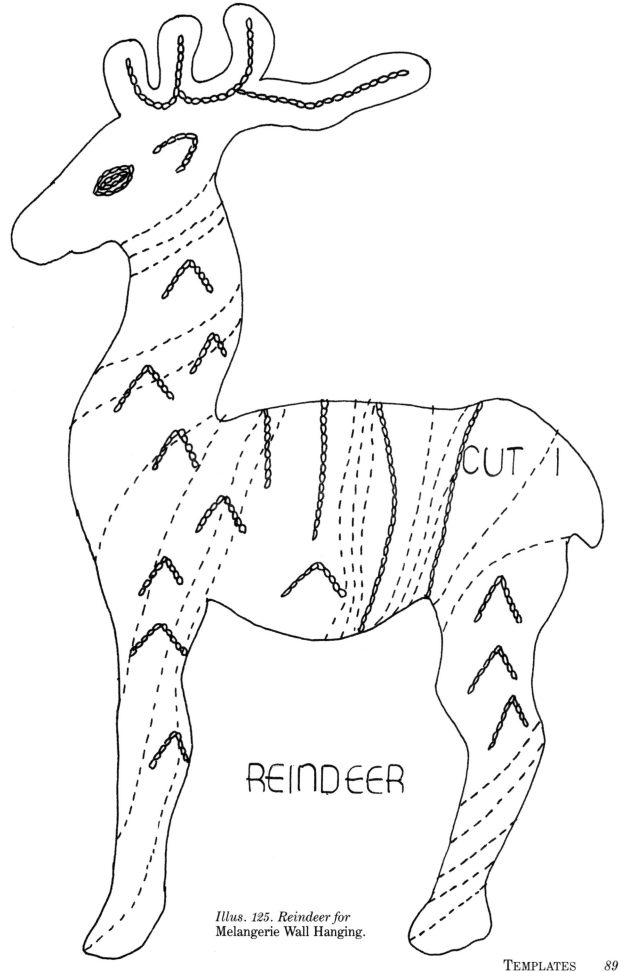

CUT 1

REINDEER

Illus. 125. Reindeer for
Melangerie Wall Hanging.

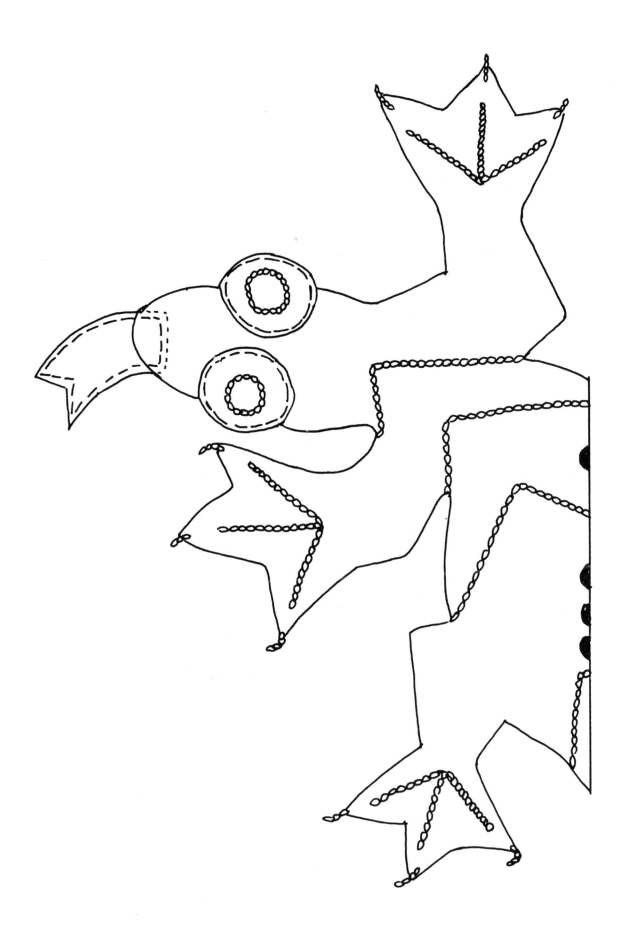

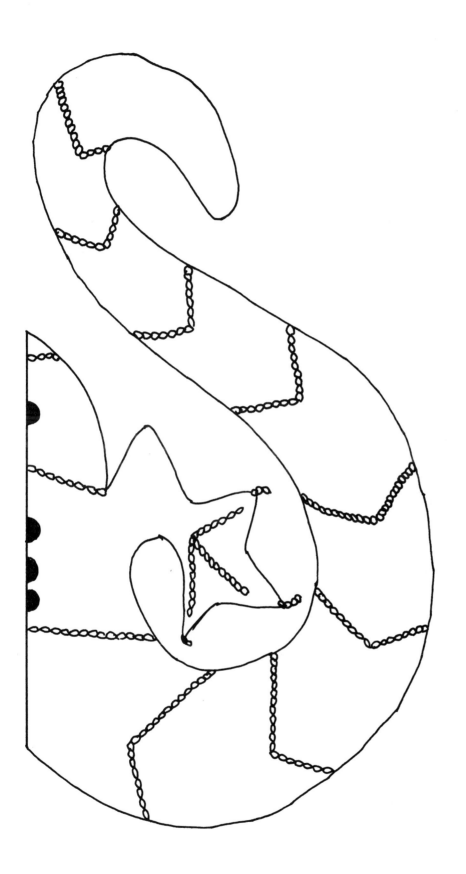

Illus. 126. Lizard for Pat's Pet Shop Quilt.

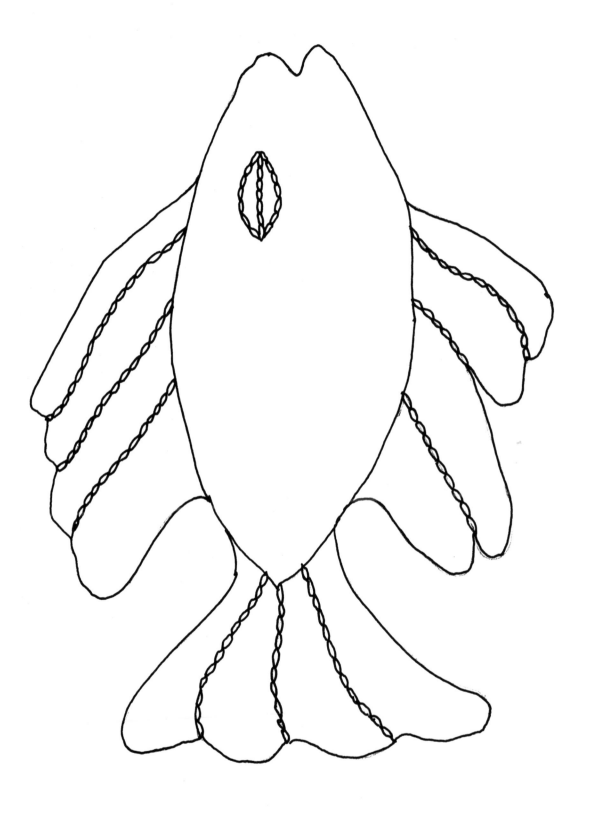

Illus. 127. Fish for Pat's Pet Shop Quilt.

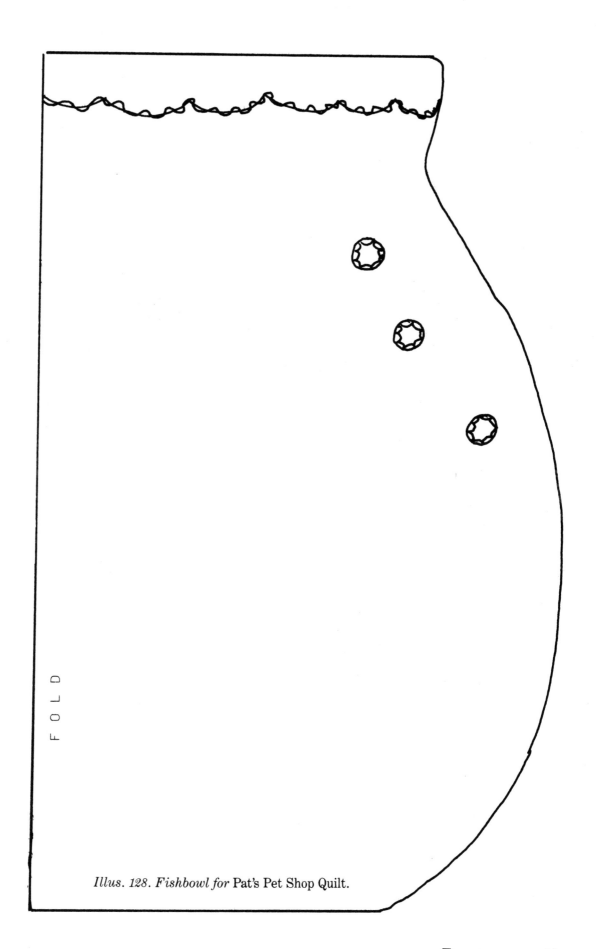

FOLD

Illus. 128. Fishbowl for Pat's Pet Shop Quilt.

Illus. 129. Cow for Dairy Checkers Quilt.

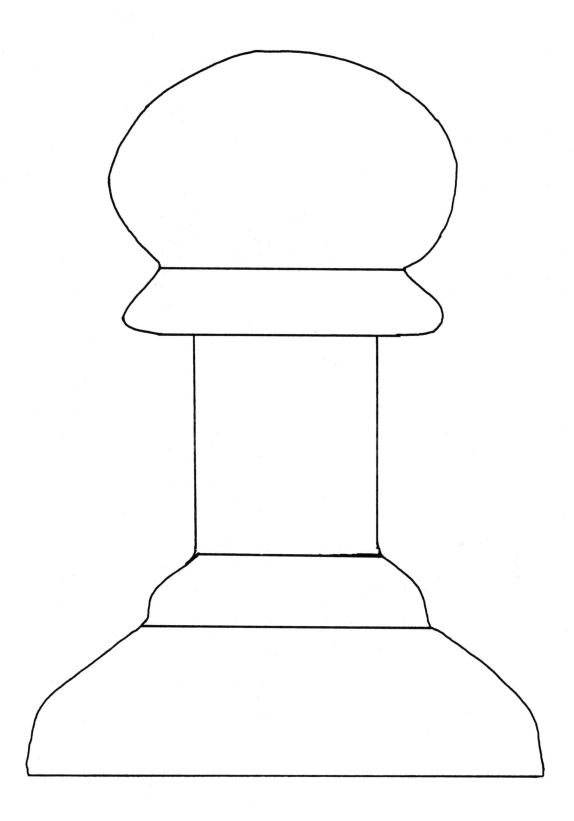

Illus. 130. Pawn for Checkmate Quilt.

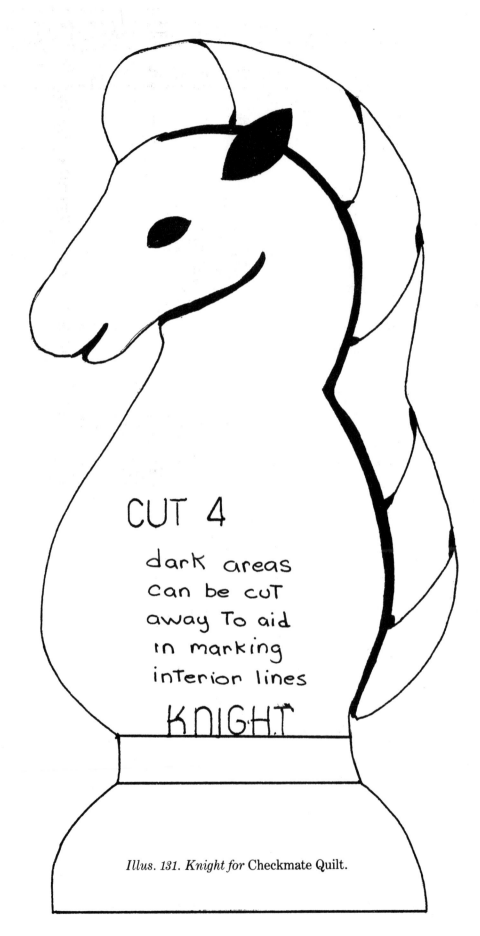

CUT 4

dark areas
can be cut
away To aid
in marking
interior lines

KNIGHT

Illus. 131. Knight for Checkmate Quilt.

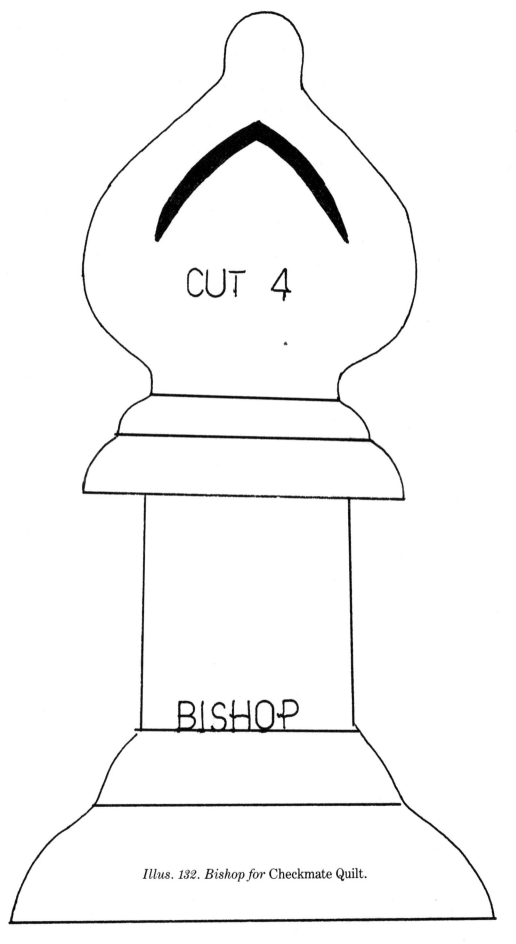

CUT 4

BISHOP

Illus. 132. Bishop for Checkmate Quilt.

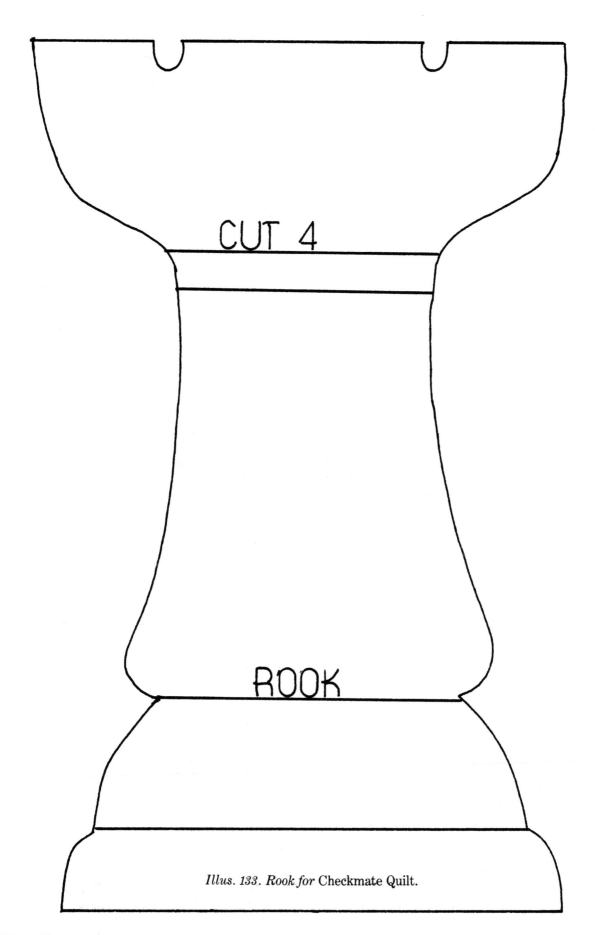

CUT 4

ROOK

Illus. 133. Rook for Checkmate Quilt.

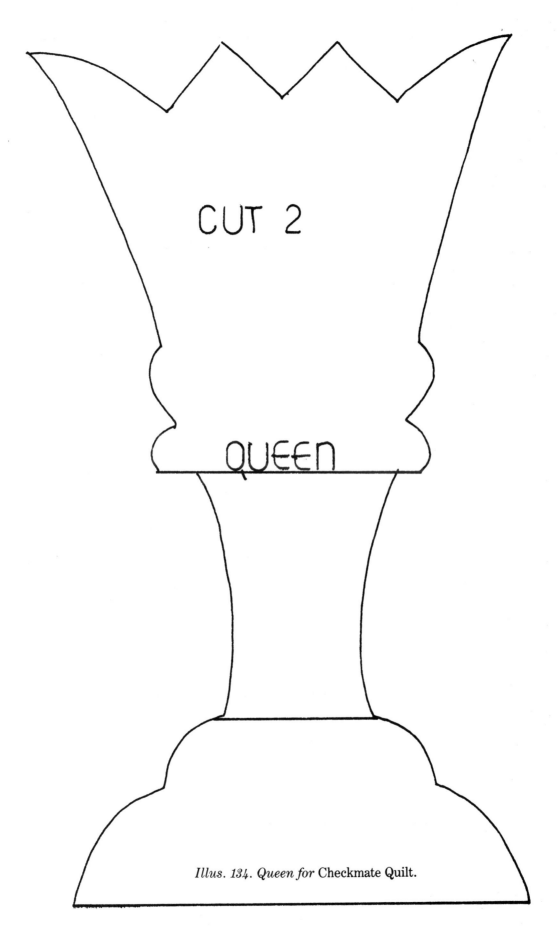

CUT 2

QUEEN

Illus. 134. Queen for Checkmate Quilt.

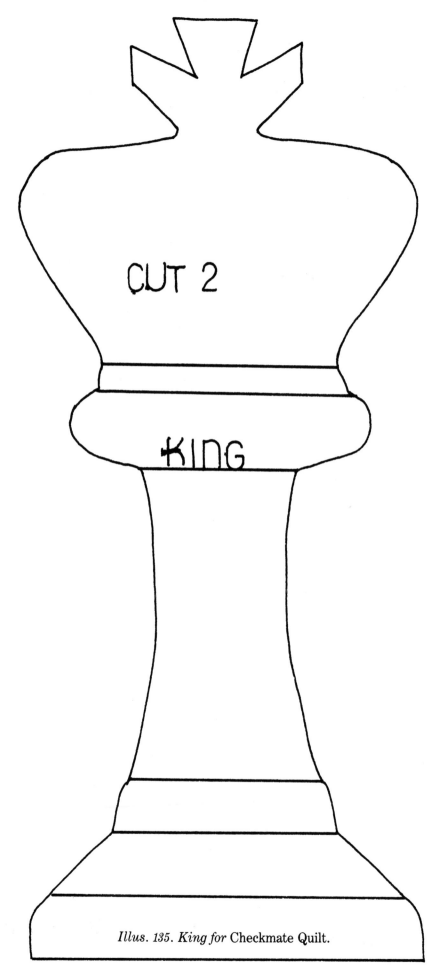

CUT 2

KING

Illus. 135. King for Checkmate Quilt.

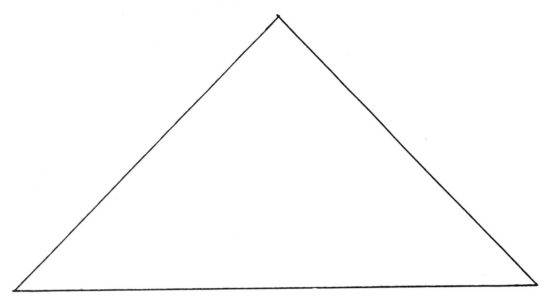

Illus. 136. (Above) Triangle template for Bear's Paw Quilt.

Illus. 137. (Below) Bear for Bear's Paw Quilt.

RHINOCEROS

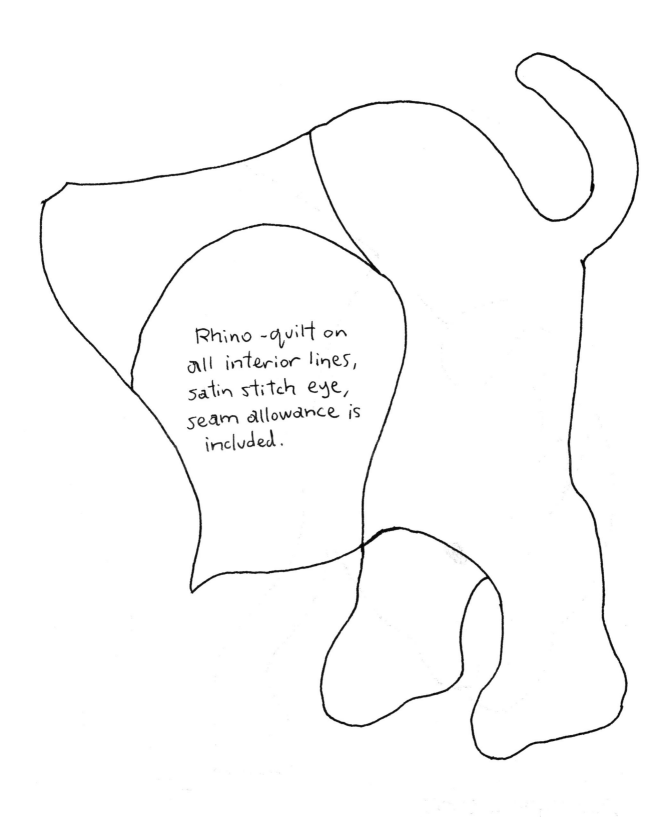

Rhino -quilt on
all interior lines,
satin stitch eye,
seam allowance is
included.

Illus. 138. Rhino for Rhinos on Record.

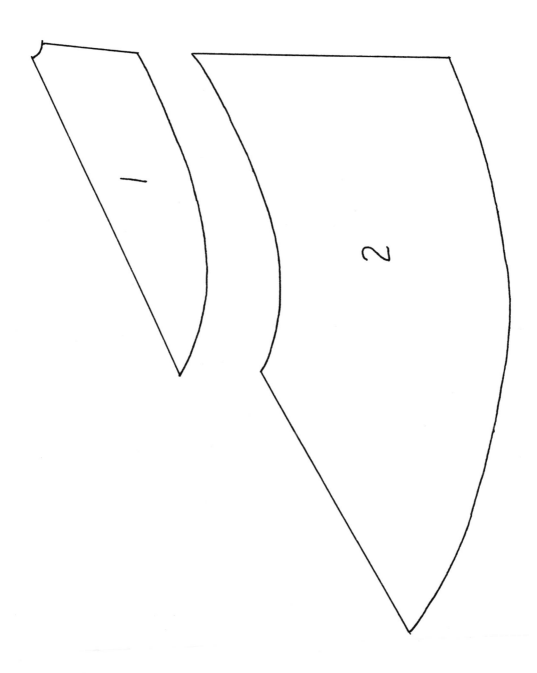

Illus. 139. Wedge #1 for Rhinos on Record.

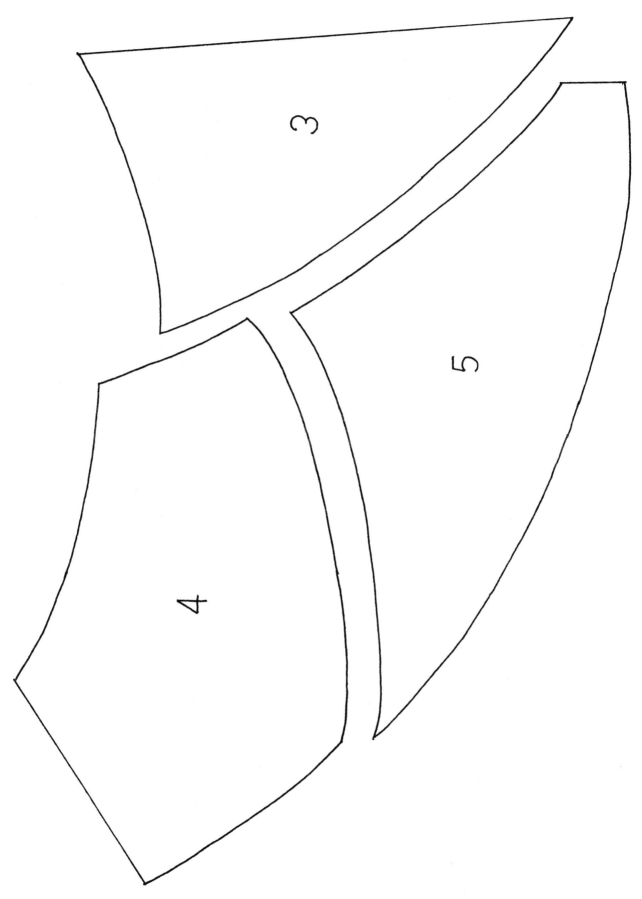

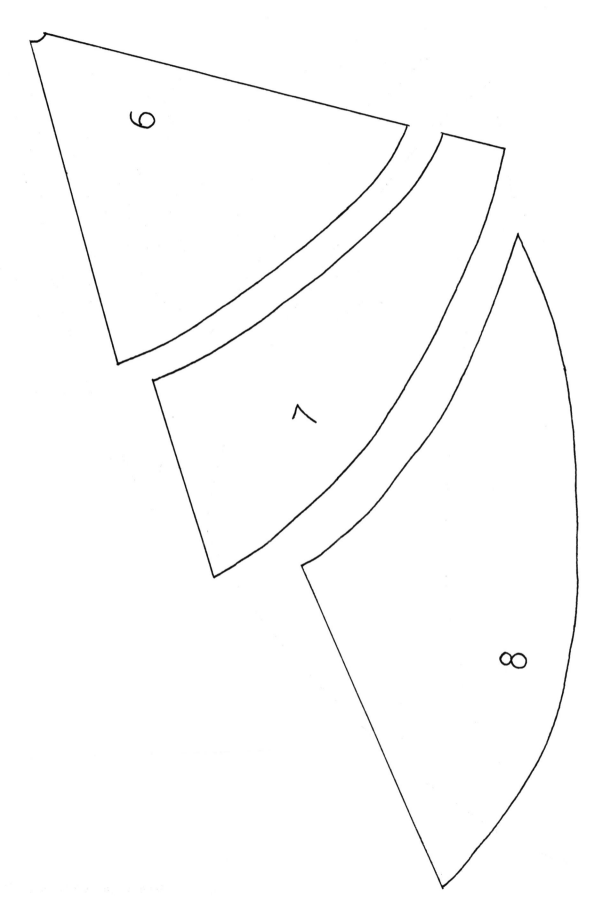

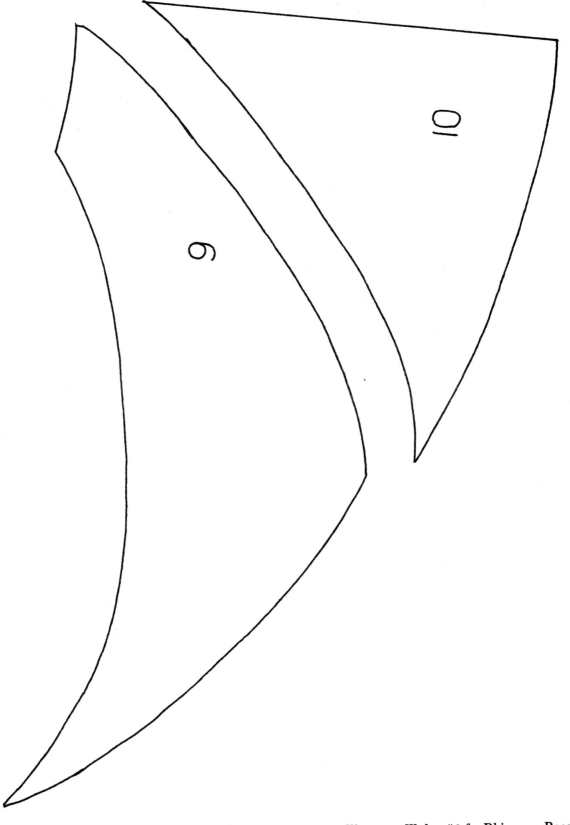

Illus. 140. Wedge #2 for Rhinos on Record.

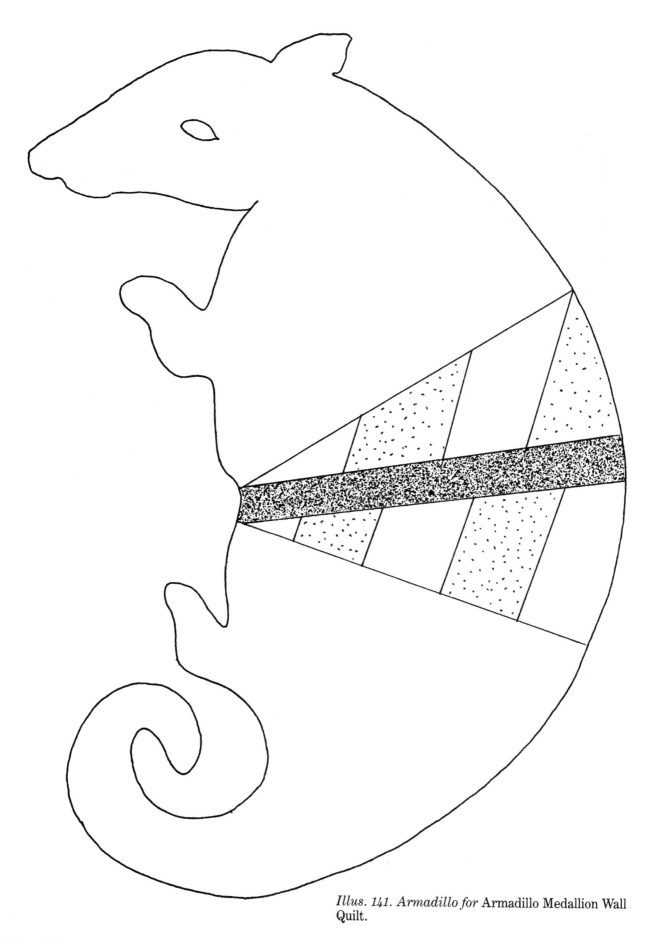

Illus. 141. Armadillo for Armadillo Medallion Wall Quilt.

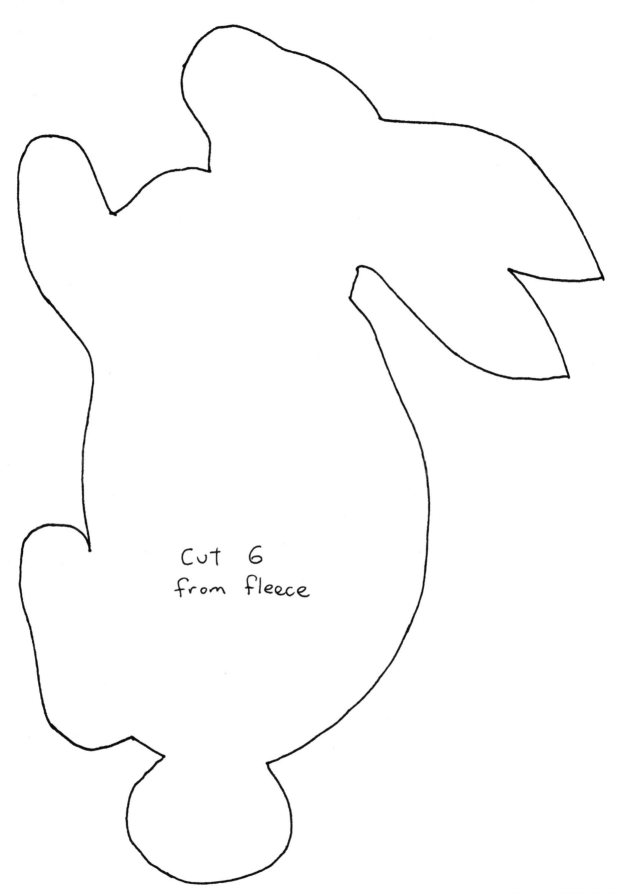

Cut 6
from fleece

Illus. 142. Bunny for Snow Bunnies Wall Quilt.

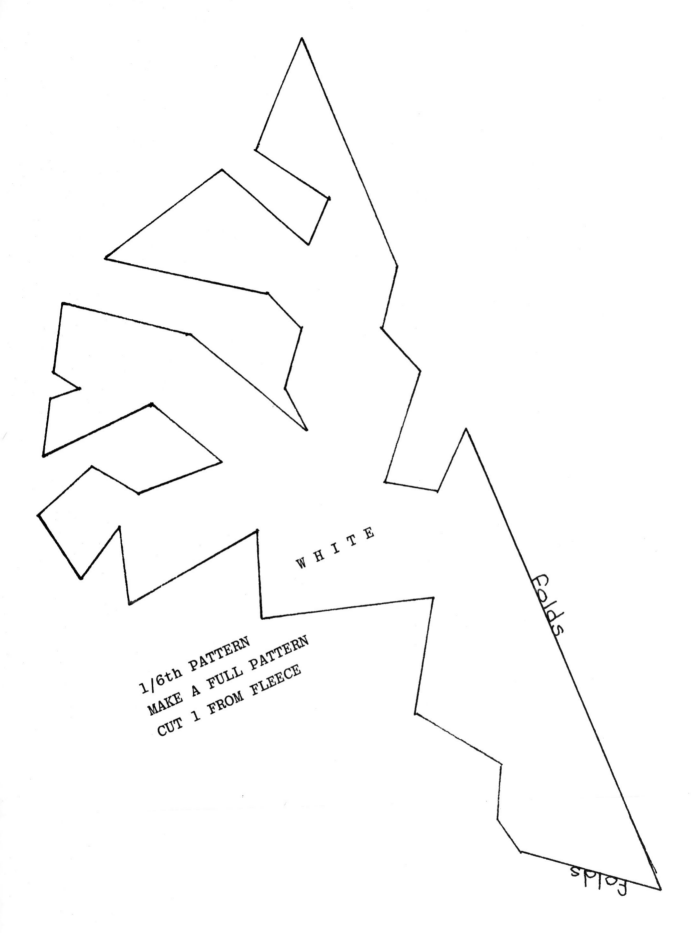

1/6th PATTERN
MAKE A FULL PATTERN
CUT 1 FROM FLEECE

WHITE

Folds

Folds

Illus. 143. Snowflake #1 for Snow Bunnies Wall Quilt.

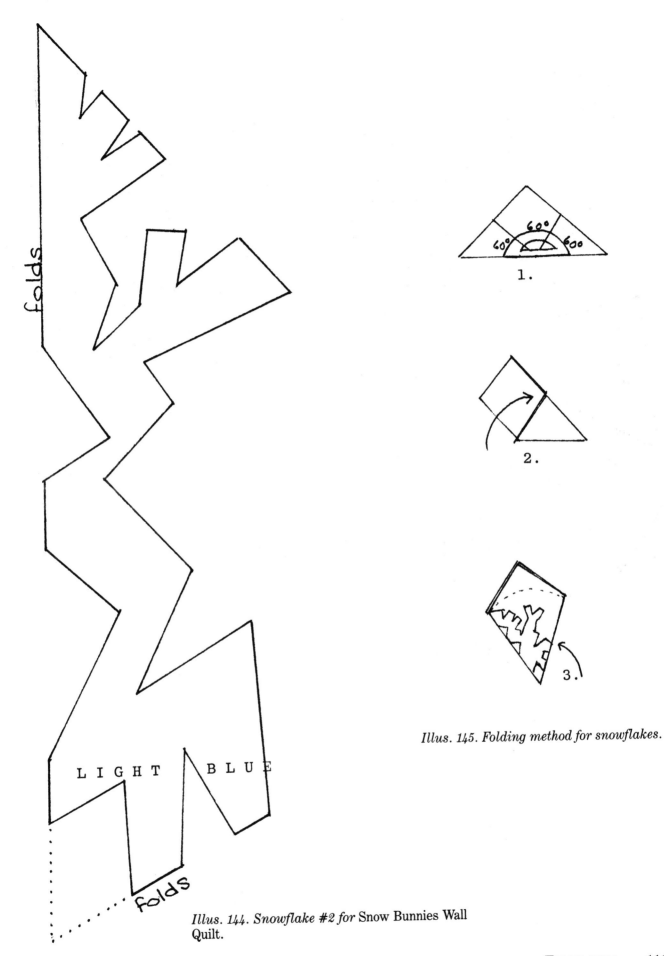

folds

folds

L I G H T   B L U E

Illus. 144. Snowflake #2 for Snow Bunnies Wall Quilt.

60° 60° 60°

1.

2.

3.

Illus. 145. Folding method for snowflakes.

Illus. 146. Quilting template for Puppy Love Wall Quilt.

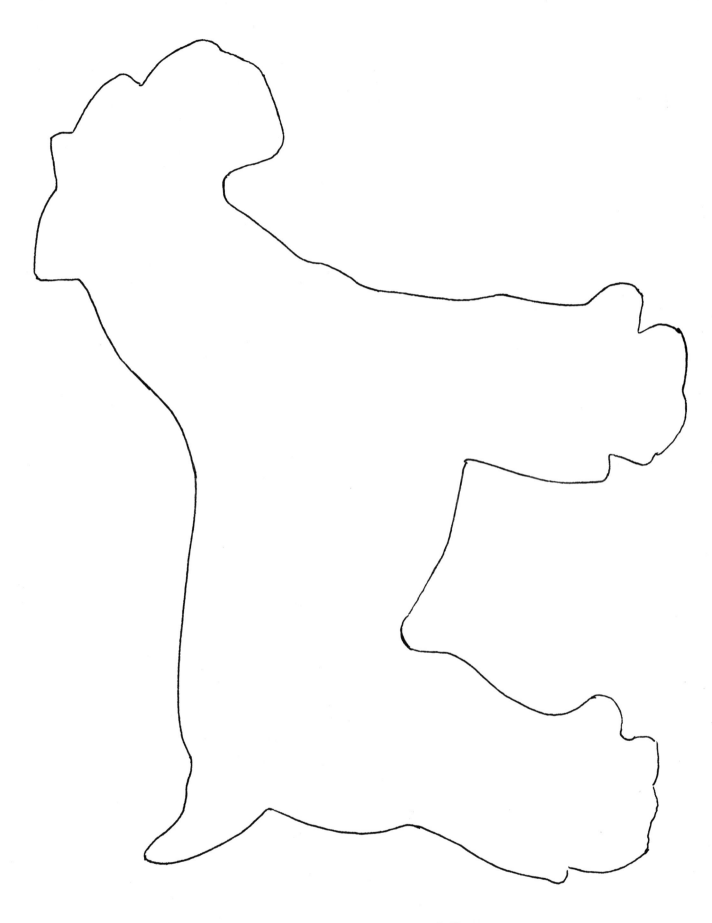

Illus. 147. Airedale for Puppy Love Wall Quilt *and* Pat's Pet Shop Quilt.

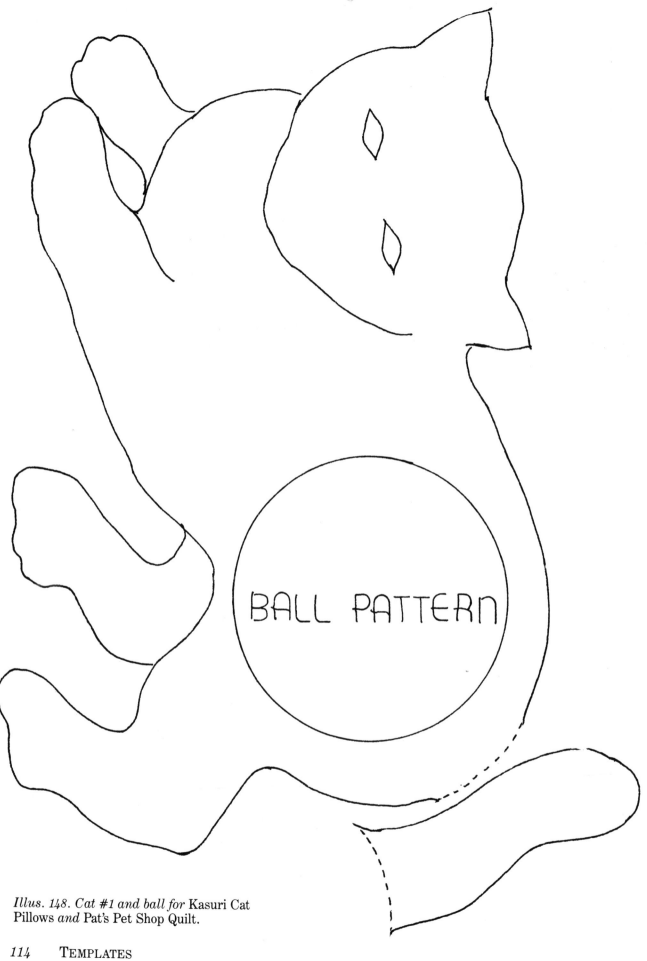

BALL PATTERN

Illus. 148. Cat #1 and ball for Kasuri Cat
Pillows *and* Pat's Pet Shop Quilt.

Illus. 149. Sashiko quilting pattern #1 for Kasuri Cat Pillows.

Illus. 150. Cat #2 for Kasuri Cat Pillows *and* Pat's Pet Shop Quilt.

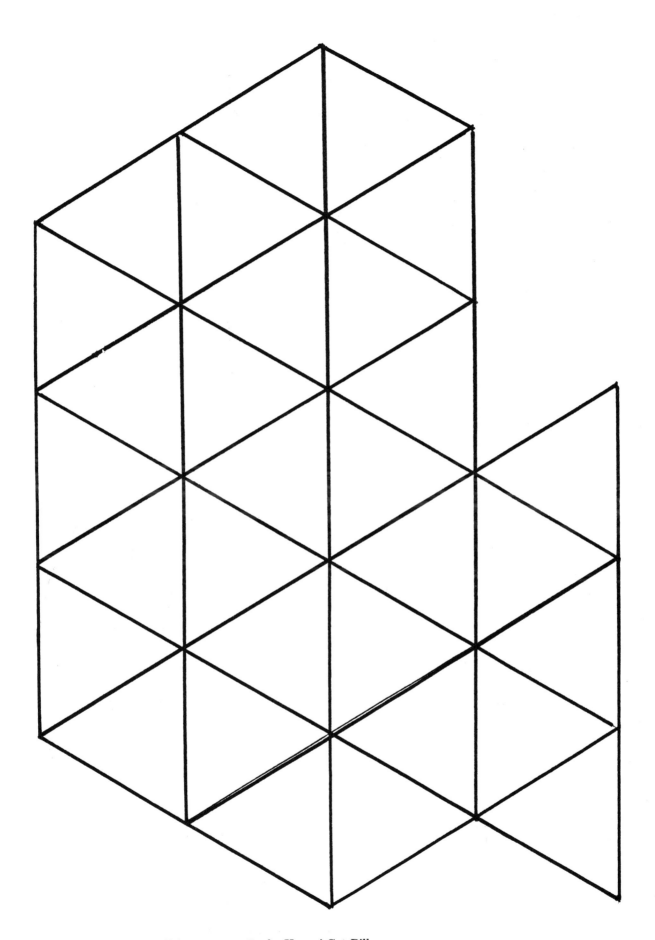

Illus. 151. Sashiko quilting pattern #2 for Kasuri Cat Pillows.

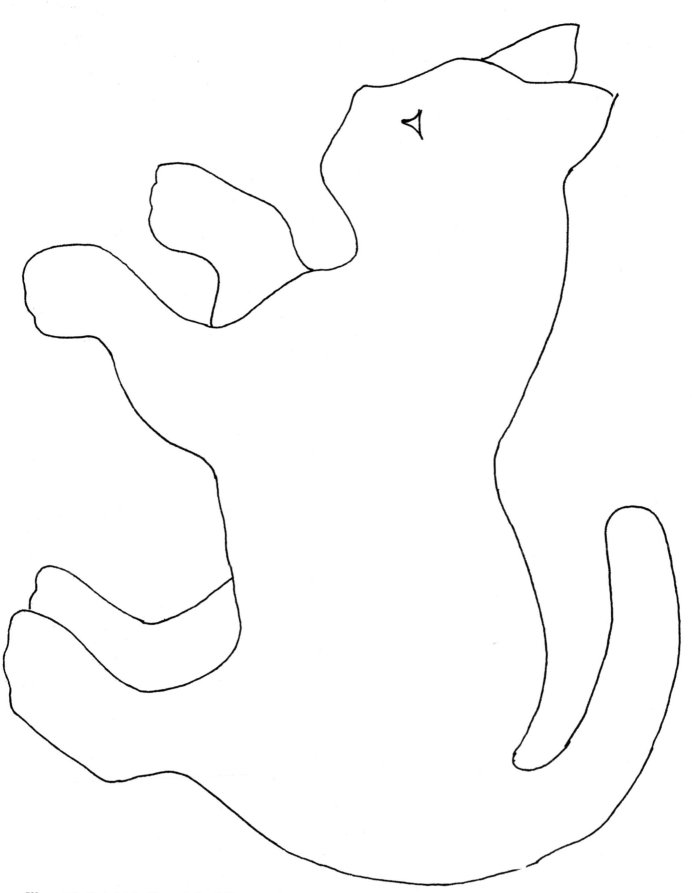

Illus. 152. Cat #3 for Kasuri Cat Pillows *and Pat's*
Pet Shop Quilt.

Illus. 153. (Opposite page) Sashiko quilting pattern
#3 for Kasuri Cat Pillows.

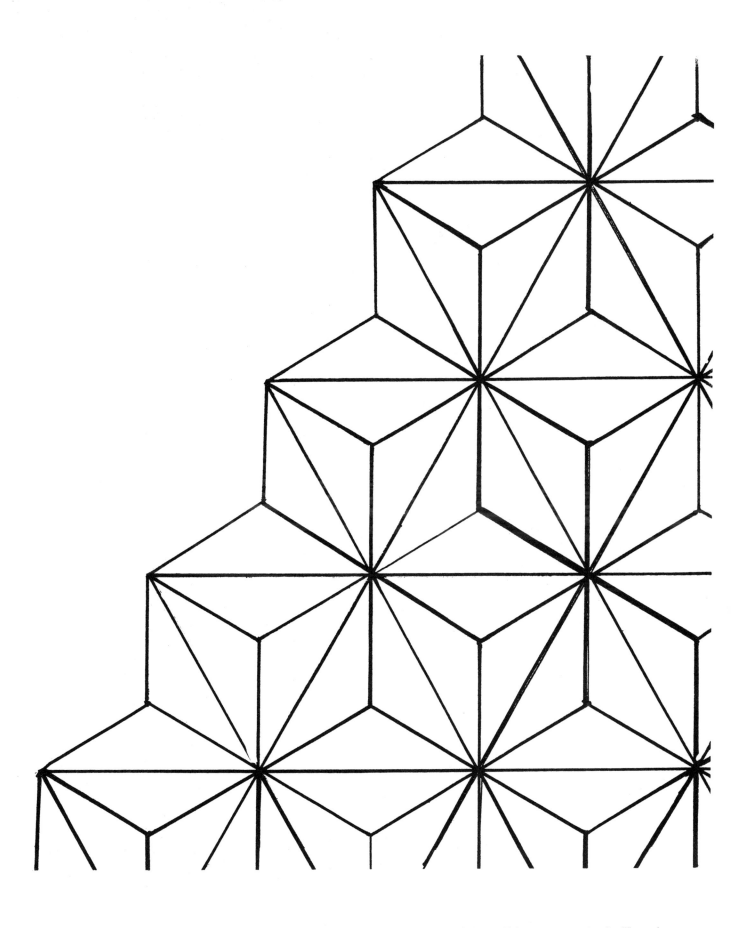

Illus. 154. (Opposite page) Cat #4 for Kasuri Cat Pillows.

Illus. 155. Sashiko quilting pattern #4 for Kasuri Cat Pillows.

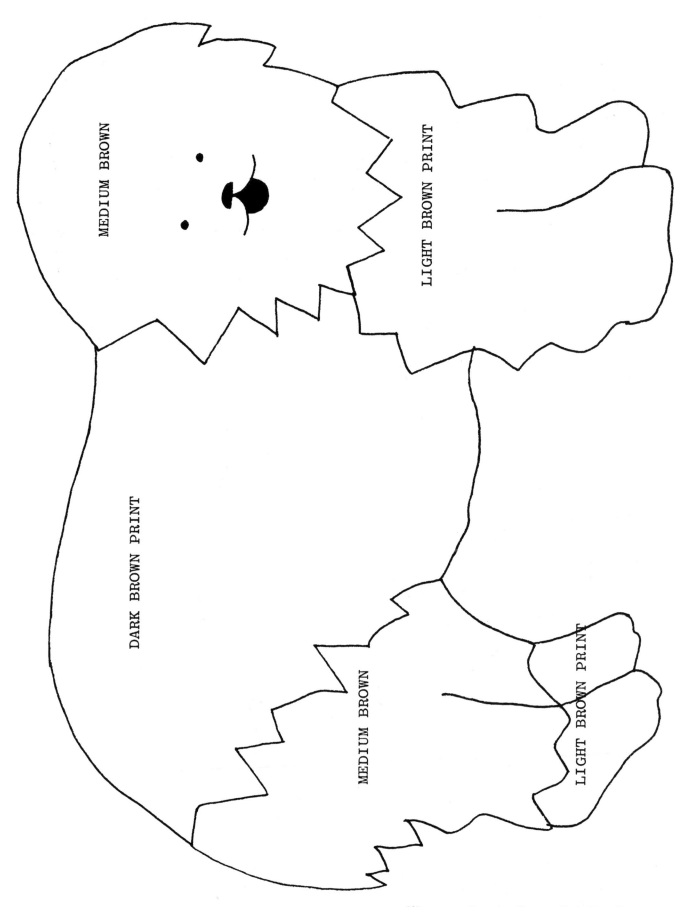

MEDIUM BROWN

LIGHT BROWN PRINT

DARK BROWN PRINT

MEDIUM BROWN

LIGHT BROWN PRINT

Illus. 156. Dog for Shaggy Dog Tote Bag.

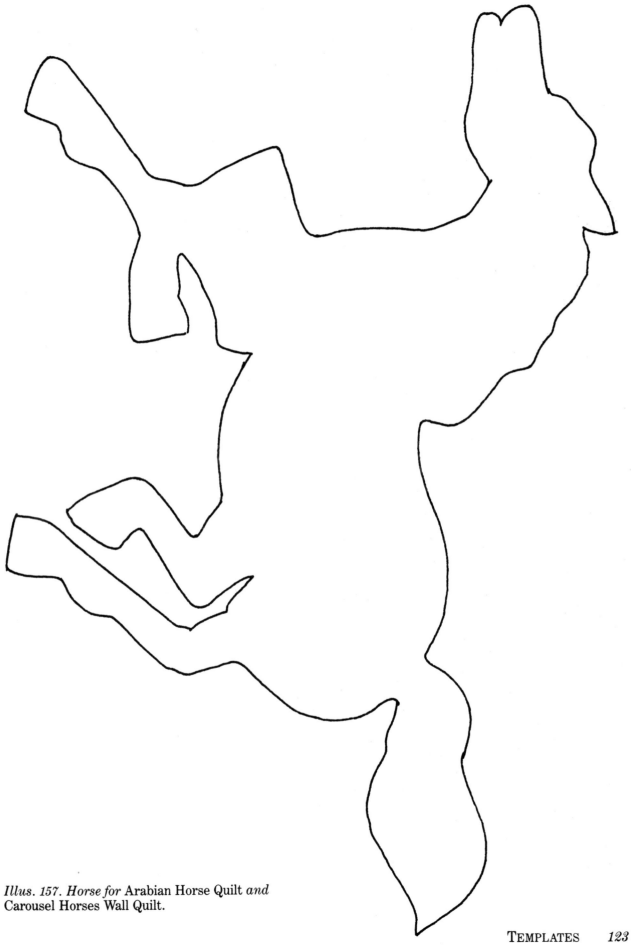

Illus. 157. Horse for Arabian Horse Quilt *and*
Carousel Horses Wall Quilt.

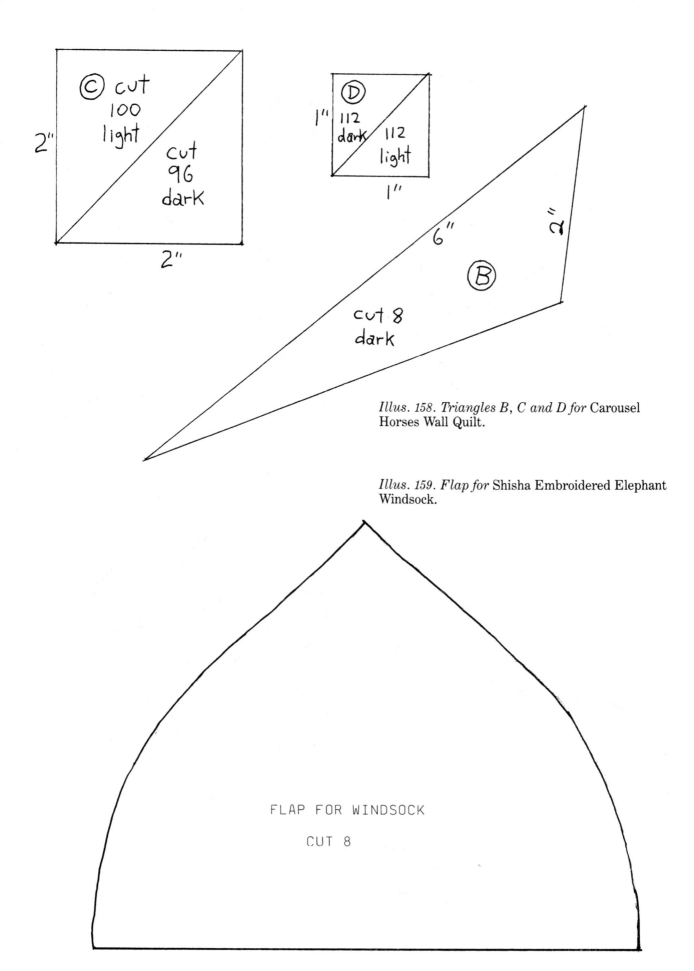

C cut 100 light
cut 96 dark
2"
2"

D 1" 112 dark 112 light
1"

6"
2"
B
cut 8 dark

Illus. 158. Triangles B, C and D for Carousel Horses Wall Quilt.

Illus. 159. Flap for Shisha Embroidered Elephant Windsock.

FLAP FOR WINDSOCK

CUT 8

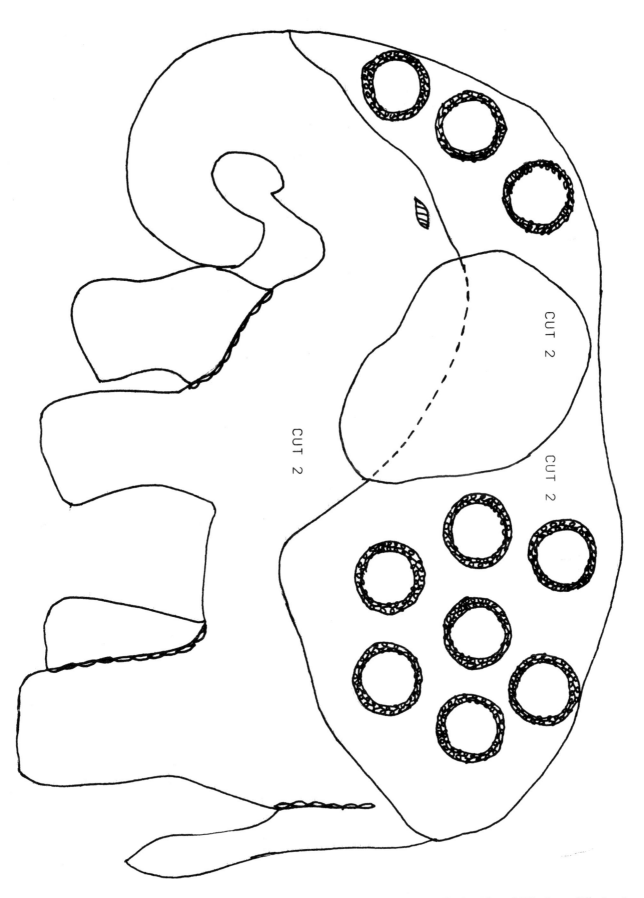

Within the illustration: CUT 2, CUT 2, CUT 2

Illus. 160. Elephant for Shisha Embroidered Elephant Windsock.

Illus. 161. Fish for Goldfish Soft Fabric Box.

Index